The Accessible Housing Design File

BARRIER *free* ENVIRONMENTS
Incorporated

VNR VAN NOSTRAND REINHOLD
New York

I(T)P™ Van Nostrand Reinhold is a division of International Thomson Publishing, Inc.
        The ITP logo is a trademark under license

Printed in the United States of America

For more information, contact:

Van Nostrand Reinhold
115 Fifth Avenue
New York, NY 10003

Chapman & Hall GmbH
Pappelallee 3
69469 Weinheim
Germany

Chapman & Hall
2-6 Boundary Row
London
SE1 8HN
United Kingdom

International Thomson Publishing Asia
221 Henderson Road #05-10
Henderson Building
Singapore 0315

Thomas Nelson Australia
102 Dodds Street
South Melbourne, 3205
Victoria, Australia

International Thomson Publishing Japan
Hirakawacho Kyowa Building, 3F
2-2-1 Hirakawacho
Chiyoda-ku, 102 Tokyo
Japan

Nelson Canada
1120 Birchmount Road
Scarborough, Ontario
Canada M1K 5G4

International Thomson Editores
Seneca 53
Col. Polanco
11560 Mexico D.F. Mexico

96 97 98 99 JDL 10 9 8 7 6 5 4

Library of Congress Cataloging-in-Publication Data

The accessible housing design file / produced by Barrier Free
   Environments Incorporated: with support from the National Institute
   on Disability and Rehabilitation Research.
        p.   cm.
    Includes index.
    ISBN 0-442-00775-2
    1. Architecture and the physically handicapped—United States.
    2. Dwellings—United States—Access for the physically handicapped.
    I. Barrier Free Environments, Inc. II. National Institute on Disability
    and Rehabilitation Research (U.S.)
    NA2545.P5A34   1991
    728'.042—dc20   90-27633
                                                          CIP

This project has been supported at least in part with funds from the United

States National Institute on Disability and Rehabilitation Research under grant

number G00863520. The content of this publication does not necessarily reflect

the views or policies of the National Institute for Disability and Rehabilitation

Research, nor does mention of trade names, commercial products, or

organizations imply endorsement by the United States Government.

CREDITS

Author

Ronald L. Mace, FAIA

Additional Contributors

James A. Bostrom

Lucy A. Harber

Leslie C. Young

Editors

Lucy A. Harber

Ellen W. Martin

Leslie C. Young

Art Director

Leslie C. Young

Graphic Artist

Kelly Houk

Illustrators

Timothy Buie

Robert B. Graham

Rex Jefferson Pace

Stephen E. Wald

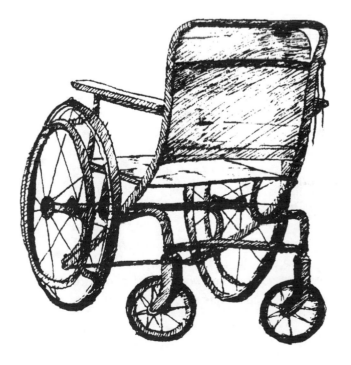

ACKNOWLEDGMENTS

This book is based upon the extensive experience of Barrier Free Environments, Inc. combined with findings from a research and demonstration project funded by the National Institute on Disability and Rehabilitation Research to investigate "Less Restrictive Housing Environments: Examples, Methods, Designs, and Guidelines for Improving New and Existing Housing" for people with disabilities. The project was conducted by Barrier Free Environments, Inc. of Raleigh, North Carolina with assistance from the following sub-contractors: Michael Jones, Ph.D., of the University of Kansas in Lawrence, Kansas; Edward Steinfeld, D.Arch. of State University of New York at Buffalo; Richard Barnes, Ph.D. of Randolph-Macon Woman's College in Lynchburg, Virginia; and Min Kantrowitz of Min Kantrowitz and Associates in Albuquerque, New Mexico.

Additional project assistance was provided by an advisory task force made up of members of the disability community, regulatory and governmental agencies, and the design and construction industry. We would like to extend our appreciation to the members of the task force who gave generously of their time to further the goals of the project. The task force members included Ellen Liberti, National Institute on Disability and Rehabilitation Research; Elaine Ostroff, Adaptive Environments Center; Katie Sloan, American Association of Retired Persons; Ravi Waldon, American Institute of Architects; Jean McGuire, Association for Retarded Citizens; Jan Sokolnicki, Cardinal Industries; Bob Ardinger, Department of Housing and Urban Development; Charles Fritts, National Apartment Association; George Genung, National Association of Home Builders; Roxane Offner, New York State Office of Advocate for the Disabled; Ron Schenewark, National Conference on Independent Living; Ruth Hall Lusher, Architectural and Transportation Barriers Compliance Board; Bob Williams, The Association for Persons with Severe Handicaps; Michael Morris, United Cerebral Palsy; and Tom Deniston, Veterans Administration.

Finally, our thanks go to the production team of Barrier Free Environments, Inc. for their fine work, cooperation, and extra effort without which this book would not have been possible.

INTRODUCTION

While the number of people with disabling conditions is enormous, neither housing which accommodates the needs of people with disabilities nor useful information on how to create it has been widely available. To date, this information has been limited to a few special researchers and designers who have developed expertise in this area through trial and error. *The Accessible Housing Design File* changes this.

The *Design File* offers a broad range of people, from professional housing designers to families and individual homeowners, a collection of widely applicable designs for accessibility which can be unobtrusively integrated into any type of new housing. These concepts, equally applicable to renovation of existing housing, improve the comfort and usefulness of homes without making them "special", "medical", "clinical", or "different". Thus, designers, homeowners, design students, specialists in aging and rehabilitation, and others involved with the design, manufacture, and construction of housing now have access to information which will help them create homes that are attractive, accommodating, and safer for the user.

In the past, building codes and standards have mandated a percentage of "special" housing for "handicapped" people. While this was an attempt to require accessible housing for people with disabilities, it perpetuated the belief that accessible housing had to be "different". Today, with the passage of legislation which includes the Fair Housing Amendments Act and the Americans with Disabilities Act, the emphasis is more appropriately on integrating into all workplaces and housing features which accommodate people with disabilities. The heightened awareness of the changing housing needs of the aging population, coupled with the increasing recognition of the civil rights of people with disabilities, is gradually resulting in changes in the way housing is designed. With the move toward more universally useable and marketable housing, the demand for easier-to-use entrances, kitchens, bedrooms, and bathrooms is being met while still demonstrating a sensitivity to aesthetics and resale value.

The *Design File* is a "how-to" manual for those interested in pursuing the ambitious and worthwhile goal of universal usability while maintaining and enhancing marketability. Each chapter offers design solutions which are clearly illustrated, extensively dimensioned, and accompanied by jargon-free explanations of why certain features are necessary to people with various levels of physical ability. Most importantly, these features are shown in the context of their setting within the house rather than as isolated elements. The *Design File's* emphasis is primarily on design for people with mobility impairments. Some information on design for people with visual and hearing impairments is included in the "Kitchens" chapter. As the research in the field of designing effective housing features for people with visual and hearing impairments develops, we hope to add additional material in this area.

To enhance the value of the book, we have referenced the national accessibility standards of the American National Standards Institute's (ANSI) Standard A117.1 (1986) and the Uniform Federal Accessibility Standards (UFAS). While some residential construction is not required to comply with these standards, we believe that knowledge of the standards will prove invaluable. For those residential projects required to meet the standards, this book will assist designers in applying creative, useful solutions as they meet or exceed the requirements. For others not held to the standards, the references to the standards still serve as a useful benchmark.

The dimensions included in the *Design File* meet or exceed ANSI and UFAS standards unless otherwise indicated. However, the *Design File* is to be used in conjunction with, not as a substitute for, the standards. While the *Design File* offers a very broad range of new and useful design solutions, given the tremendous variations in state and local requirements, it is well beyond the scope of the book to ensure compliance with all possible codes and standards. The user must rely on the local, state, or national requirements having jurisdiction and not on the supplemental information contained in the *Design File.*

The information contained in the book is derived from many sources including national accessibility standards; Barrier Free Environments' seventeen years experience in designing houses, commercial spaces, and products for people with disabilities; our vast network of advisors in the field of disability; selected literature; and the findings of a research project on accessible housing sponsored by the National Institute on Disability and Rehabilitation Research. We are very excited about the opportunity to bring the results of our housing design experiences and findings, in a clear and easy-to-use format, to both the providers and users of accessible homes.

Copies of ANSI A117.1 are available from:

American National Standards Institute, Inc.

1430 Broadway

New York, NY 10018

Copies of UFAS are available from:

Architectural and Transportation Barriers

Compliance Board

1111 18th Street, NW, Suite 501

Washington, DC 20036

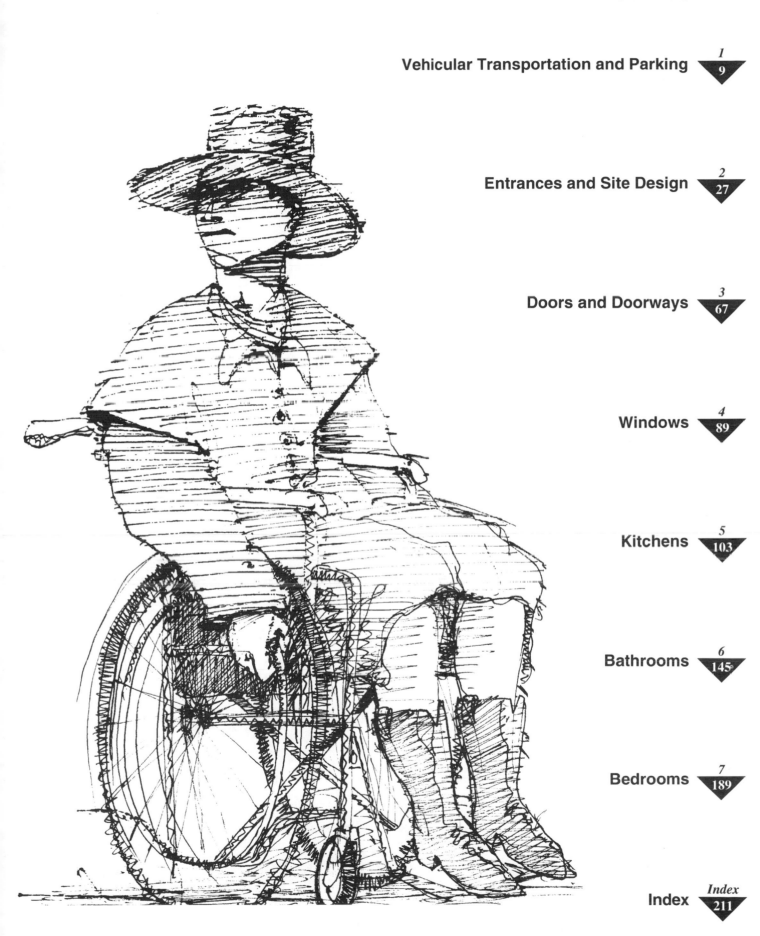

CHAPTERS

▲

CHAPTER 1

Vehicular transportation ▼ 9
and parking

▲

Accessible Transportation

Accessible transportation is of vital importance for disabled people, perhaps more so than for able-bodied people, because it helps a disabled person overcome the common problems of reduced strength and stamina as they take part in events and activities outside their homes. However, the design of most standard vehicles makes transportation for people with mobility impairments (people who use wheelchairs, canes, crutches, or walkers) somewhat more difficult than for other people. This difficulty arises from everyday causes. First, the disabled person's inability to safely climb steps, a necessity for boarding most types of mass transit; second, obstacles encountered when attempting to transfer into a vehicle without standing and/or walking; and third, their space requirements for loading and transporting wheelchairs, walkers and other mobility aids.

To overcome these difficulties, specially equipped cars, vans, and buses are commonly used by people with mobility impairments. Appropriate parking spaces, drop-off areas, garages, and boarding shelters should be planned as part of all housing to facilitate the use of these types of transportation.

Two-door Cars with Wide Doors Have Room to Make Transfer

Vehicle Types and Use
Cars

All types and sizes of cars are used by disabled people, their families, and friends but mid-sized or full-sized cars are the most common because they provide enough space in which to place and transport a wheelchair or walker. Many mobility impaired people, including those who use wheelchairs, drive cars that are equipped with hand controls, power brakes, power steering, and other safety and assist features such as automatic transmissions. Two-door models are the most useful because the doors are large and provide easy access to the front seats. The larger two-door models also provide easier access to the space behind the front seat where folded wheelchairs and walkers can be placed.

Many wheelchair users who drive transfer from the wheelchair to the car seat, fold up their wheelchair, and lift the chair into the car behind the front seat. Others, who are unable to manage this task, may have someone else fold up the chair and place it inside the car, in the trunk, or possibly in a rack on the back or the top of the car. When taxi cabs pick up mobility impaired people, the driver may be required to help load the wheelchair or walker.

And Pull Folded Chair in Behind Driver's Seat

Vehicle Types and Use
Cars

People who use powered wheelchairs generally do not use cars for transportation or use them much less frequently. Most powered wheelchairs are not easily disassembled and some do not fold. All have heavy batteries which must be disconnected and removed before they can be stowed in a car. This process is usually too awkward and difficult to accomplish for frequent short trips.

There are some special lifts or racks that allow powered chairs and scooters to be hung outside the car on the rear bumper. These devices may suffice for short trips but are not adequate for long distances or bad weather. The major limitation of the exterior rear-mounted chairlift or rack is that it cannot be used independently unless the disabled user can walk the short distance from the lift to the car door. Therefore, most powered wheelchair users will require assistance to load the chair after they have transferred into the car seat and assistance to retrieve it upon arrival at their destination.

Rear-mounted Wheelchair Transport Lift

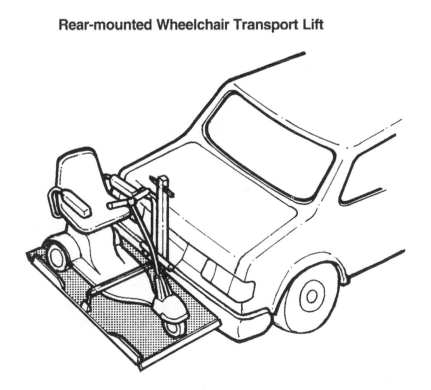

Vehicle Types and Use

Vans

Vans are a popular and effective choice of transportation especially for people who use powered wheelchairs and often for people who use manual wheelchairs. Adapted vans are commonly equipped with mechanical lifts, automatic doors, boarding ramps, raised roofs, and lowered floors, to make it possible for a person to remain in their wheelchair while boarding, riding, and even driving. Some vans even have special suspension systems that lower the van to make it easier to enter or exit. The interior of vans can be equipped with safety tie-down devices for wheelchairs, hand controls, special motor-powered seats, and a variety of other features to make transportation easy, safe, and enjoyable.

Either full-sized or mini vans can be adapted to suit the individual user. The choice of the size and other equipment depends on the number of people who will use it, the abilities of the disabled user, and the type and size of the user's mobility device(s). Vans equipped with lifts are most popular with individuals and families because of their ease of use. Side-mounted lifts are the most common. Access to vans can be provided through either the passenger side cargo doors or the rear doors.

Vans with folding manually operated ramps are used by many cab companies because they are less expensive and require no maintenance. Drivers must manually assist the wheelchair user to safely negotiate the inclined ramp and once inside, secure the wheelchair for transport.

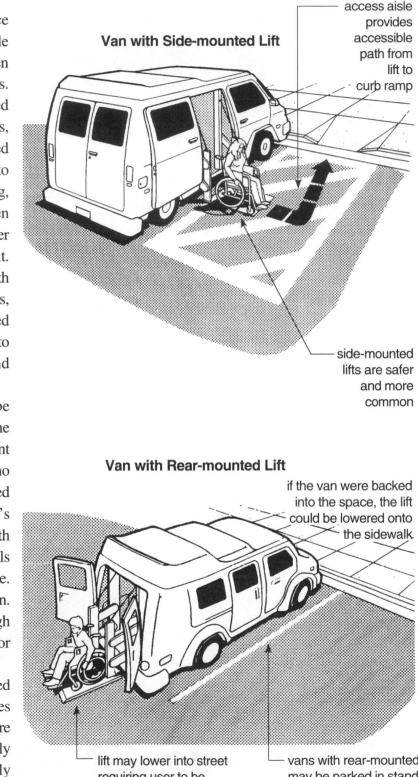

Van with Side-mounted Lift

access aisle provides accessible path from lift to curb ramp

side-mounted lifts are safer and more common

Van with Rear-mounted Lift

if the van were backed into the space, the lift could be lowered onto the sidewalk

lift may lower into street requiring user to be extra cautious to avoid being hit by oncoming traffic

vans with rear-mounted lifts may be parked in standard spaces since access aisle is not needed (however a safe route to sidewalk must be provided)

Vehicle Types and Use
Bus Service

In many communities, public bus services provide accessible transportation by equipping mainline passenger buses with wheelchair lifts or by operating special door-to-door services using smaller buses or vans. Such transit services are not available or successfully usable in all localities but may be expected to improve as current and pending federal law requires equal access to public services.

Lifts on buses are used to board people using wheelchairs and others who cannot climb the high steps that are common on buses. Smaller special service buses and some school buses are also similarly equipped. Accessible buses have a limited number of parking spaces allocated for wheelchairs which are equipped with tie down mechanisms. The bus driver operates the lift and engages the tie down mechanisms for all passengers requiring this type of boarding assistance.

Accessible Public Bus with Wheelchair Lift

Parking Spaces

Because disabled people drive vehicles that are standard sizes, standard 8'-0" or 9"-0" parking spaces are adequate if a clear access aisle is provided on at least one side of each space. In covered parking areas, additional overhead clearance may be required to accommodate vans with raised roofs. An overhead clearance of at least 9'-6" should be allotted.

Accessible Parking Includes Standard Space Plus Access Aisle

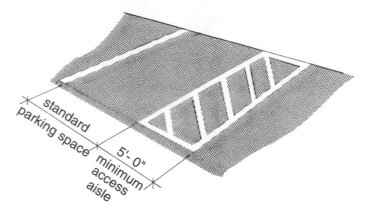

Parking Spaces

Access Aisles at Parking Spaces

The clear space required beside accessible parking spaces is called an access aisle. The national and federal standards for accessibility, as well as most state codes, require access aisles to be at the level of the parking surface, be at least 5'-0" wide, and be the full length of the parking space.

The access aisles must connect with an accessible route such as a sidewalk, walkway, or other pedestrian path that leads to the facility entrances (see the description of accessible routes in "Site and Entrances" in the *Design File).* The 5'-0" access aisle width provides space for lowering lift platforms, swinging car doors open, and maneuvering wheelchairs and walkers while boarding vehicles. Where multiple parking spaces are provided, one access aisle can serve two spaces.

Two Parking Spaces May Share One Access Aisle

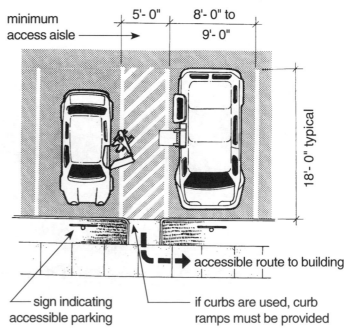

where multiple parking spaces are provided, one access aisle can serve two spaces

Alternate Method for Providing Accessible Parking

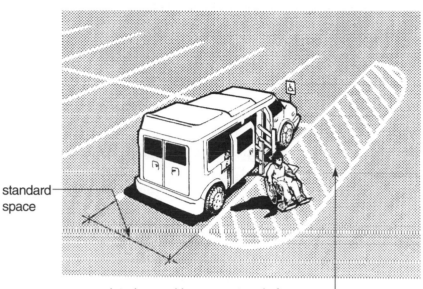

standard space

painted no parking area at end of rows can function as an access aisle and provide more wheelchair maneuvering space than the 5' aisle

Parking Spaces
Access Aisles at Parking Spaces

The 5'-0" access aisle width is regarded as a minimum and is too narrow for comfortable use of some lifts which may extend up to 4'-0" from the vehicles. Wider access aisles are thus preferred and should be included when possible. As shown in the accompanying illustration, additional maneuvering space can be provided at no extra cost by locating some accessible spaces at the ends of rows where open space may already be required.

Surfaces at Parking Spaces Must Not Be Sand, Gravel, or Other Loose Materials

Parking Spaces
Surfaces at Accessible Parking Spaces

Ground surfaces for parking spaces, access aisles, and accessible routes are best if paved with hard surface materials such as concrete, brick, or asphalt. Where paving is not possible, crushed stone, sandstone, and other materials that compact into relatively smooth dense surfaces can also be used. Gravel, sand, earth, and similar materials that are soft or loose must not be used because many people who walk with difficulty or who use wheelchairs cannot move across such surfaces.

Parking Spaces

Ground Slope at Accessible Parking Spaces and Access Aisles

Accessible parking spaces and access aisles should be as level as possible to make wheelchair maneuvering easier. If a ground slope is unavoidable, it should be parallel to either the length or width of the parking space. A diagonal or multiple cross slope is extremely difficult to maneuver and should be avoided.

Slopes should be limited to a maximum of 1" rise or drop for every 50" of run/length. Gentle slopes are required as parking spaces with steep slopes make it difficult for people to open or close their doors or position their lifts.

Level Parking Spaces Are Required

if slope is too steep, it is impossible for some disabled people to safely get to the space as well as in or out of their car

slope should not exceed 1" in 50"

Parking Spaces

Curbs at Accessible Parking Spaces

Level Parking Spaces with Smooth Transition to Access Route Are Preferred

Parking spaces, access aisles, and adjacent sidewalks and walkways are most useable if they are at a common level. These elements should not be separated by curbs or any abrupt changes of level greater than 1/4". If curbs are used on the site, they must be omitted at access aisles and curb ramps installed to provide access.

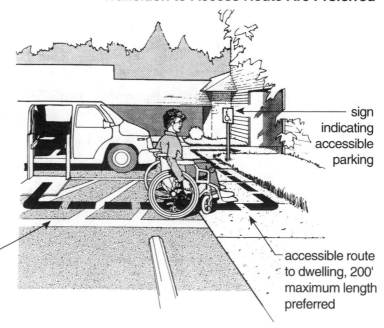

sign indicating accessible parking

parking space and access aisle (5' wide minimum) should have little or no slope

accessible route to dwelling, 200' maximum length preferred

When accessible routes such as sidewalks are placed at the same level as the parking surface, wheel stops, bollards, posts, or other devices must be installed to prevent parked cars from encroaching on the access route.

If curbs or changes in level are unavoidable, curb ramps or sloping surfaces at access aisles should have a maximum slope of 1" rise for every 12" of run. Curb ramps should be recessed into curbs rather than projecting out into traffic or parking lanes. Two types of recessed curb ramps are commonly used in a variety of applications.

The "flared curb" ramp is safest and allows people to enter the ramp directly or from a side angle. This design is best used where pedestrians are likely to walk across the ramp.

The "returned curb" ramp has the curb "turned back" the full depth of the ramp. This design can be a tripping hazard to pedestrians and should be used only where adjacent plant beds or other features will prevent approach from the sides.

Walk Width Must Be Maintained

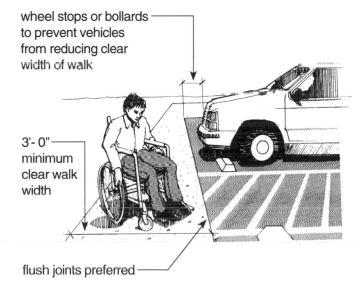

wheel stops or bollards to prevent vehicles from reducing clear width of walk

3'- 0" minimum clear walk width

flush joints preferred

Flared Curb Ramp

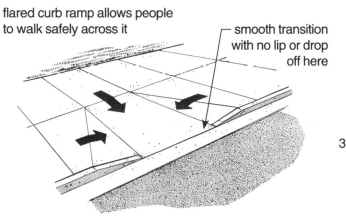

flared curb ramp allows people to walk safely across it

smooth transition with no lip or drop off here

Returned Curb Ramp

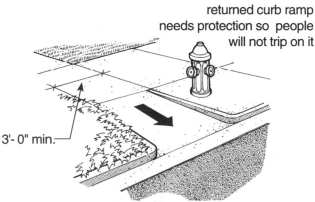

returned curb ramp needs protection so people will not trip on it

3'- 0" min.

Parking Spaces

Curbs at Accessible Parking Spaces

Curb ramps that extend out from curbs into parking spaces, traffic lanes, or access aisles are not acceptable. They interfere with drainage, are frequently run over by vehicles and, when placed in access aisles, create awkward sloping surfaces that interfere with access to front passenger doors on some vehicles and side-mounted lifts on vans.

Extended Curb Ramps Interfere with Van Lifts and Access to Front Door of Cars and Should Not Be Installed

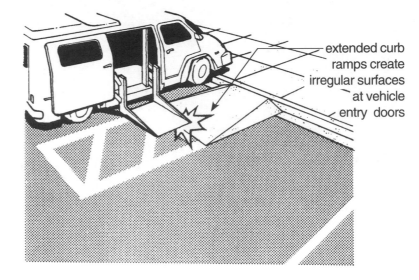

extended curb ramps create irregular surfaces at vehicle entry doors

Recessed Curb Ramps Leave the Access Aisle Clear and Are Preferred

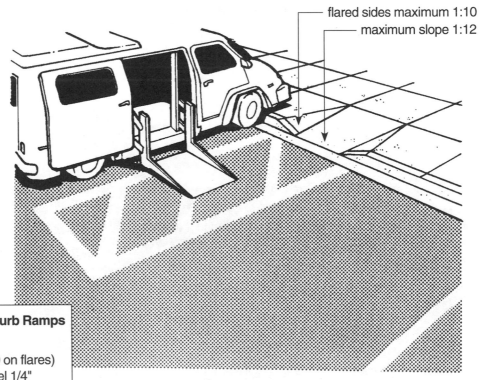

flared sides maximum 1:10
maximum slope 1:12

General Characteristics for Curb Ramps

Minimum width 3'- 0"
Maximum slope 1 in 12 (1 in 10 on flares)
Maximum abrupt change in level 1/4"

Passenger Drop-off Area Outside Traffic Lanes

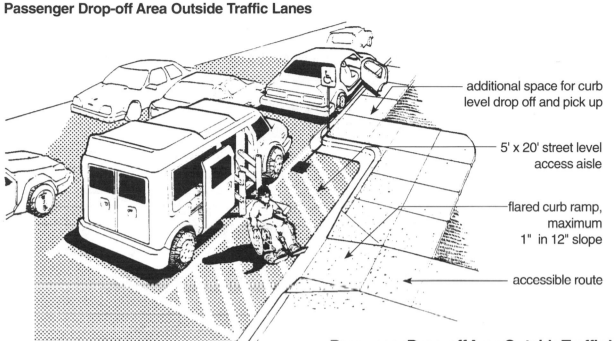

additional space for curb level drop off and pick up

5' x 20' street level access aisle

flared curb ramp, maximum 1" in 12" slope

accessible route

Passenger Drop-off Area Outside Traffic Lanes

Many people with disabilities require extra time to board and exit vehicles because of the need to transfer into seats, load wheelchairs or walkers, or use wheelchair lifts. To accommodate this need, drop-off spaces should be located near accessible entrances but out of traffic lanes so that boarding or exiting can occur without disrupting the flow of other vehicular or pedestrian traffic.

Passenger drop-off and pick-up areas should have access aisles adjacent and parallel to the vehicle pull-up space. These access aisles should be at least 5' wide by 20' long to provide maneuvering space for people using wheelchairs and walkers as they board and exit vehicles. A curb ramp or level path must connect the access aisle with an accessible route or walkway that leads to the building entrance.

Some people enter their vehicles best from a curb height while others can only board from street level. To accommodate this, it is best if drop-off areas provide both curbed and non-curbed options.

Some People Can Best Board from Curb Level

Carports and Garages

Shelter for Boarding

Since most people with disabilities require more time to get in and out of vehicles, whenever possible it is best to provide some type of shelter over parking and boarding spaces. It is particularly difficult for mobility impaired people to use umbrellas, rain coats and other protective gear. These factors combined with the additional time needed for boarding, can preclude transportation on inclement days—a condition that potentially interferes with employment, education, and recreation. For many people, sheltered parking is absolutely necessary to maintain independence during bad weather.

Shelter also keeps snow, ice, and frost off of vehicles during the winter, eliminating the need to scrape the windshield, a task that may be difficult or impossible for some drivers. Also, some people with disabilities have conditions that make them sensitive to extremes of temperature or air movement. When possible, shelter should also provide protection from direct sun, extreme cold, and high wind conditions.

Carports and garages can be designed and built to provide adequate shelter. These structures may need to be larger than the standard carport or garage because of the raised roofs on some vans and the need for an access aisle to accommodate lifts or open car doors.

Shelter for Boarding

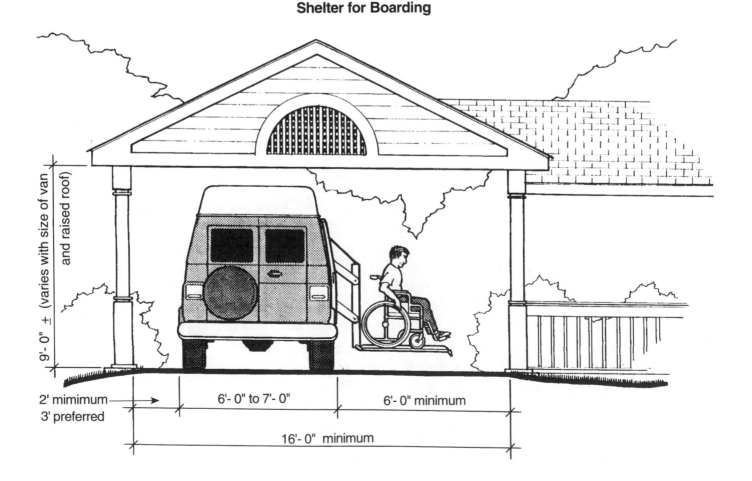

Garage for Van Plus Access Aisle to House

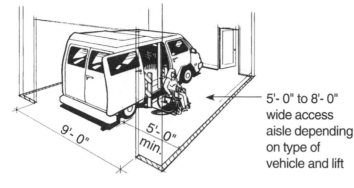

9'- 0"

5'- 0" min.

5'- 0" to 8'- 0" wide access aisle depending on type of vehicle and lift

Garage for Van and Car Plus Access Aisle to House

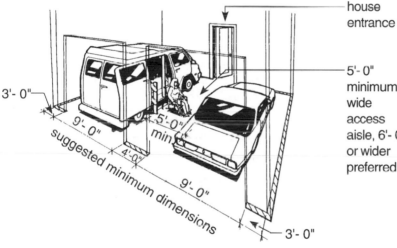

3'- 0"

9'- 0"

suggested minimum dimensions

4'- 0"

5'- 0" min.

9'- 0"

3'- 0"

house entrance

5'- 0" minimum wide access aisle, 6'- 0" or wider preferred

Carports and Garages
Floor Size

Floor area for parking structures is based on standard vehicle dimensions, the number of vehicles to be stored, plus minimum 5'-0" wide access aisles beside or between the vehicles. Shown in the accompanying illustrations are some examples of typical floor plans for accessible garages. The designer or builder of accessible homes should provide ample additional space for accessible routes as well as the storage space which is common in all garages.

Carports and Garages
Overhead Clearance

Cars, mini vans, and full-sized vans not equipped with raised roofs will generally fit in parking structures having conventional ceiling heights and entrance doors. Full-sized vans and some mini vans, when equipped with raised roofs, will not.

Some raised roof vans may be as high as 8'-0" or more. Allowing at least 6" for clearance, door opening height and/or ceiling heights may need to be 9'-0"±. Note, however, that vehicle heights vary widely and it is best to check carefully on the exact vehicles to be used before establishing a minimum overhead clearance for a project.

Overhead Clearance

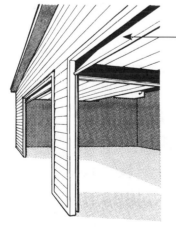

The garage door often hangs down in the opening even when the door is fully open reducing the clear height.

**Step Prevents Fumes from
Entering House but Limits Access**

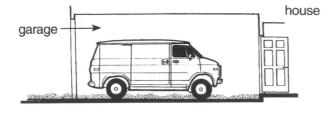

**Accessible Sloped Floor
Prevents Fumes from Entering House**

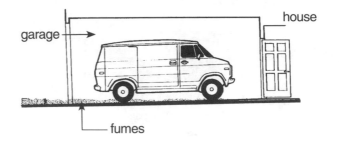

Carports and Garages

Changes in Level in Garages

Some building codes require garage floor levels to be several inches below the house floor level when the garage is attached to the house. This requirement is intended to prevent the fumes, from leaking and/or spilled fuel, from drifting into the dwelling. The change in level creates a step which prevents the heavier-than-air fumes from passing through the connecting door into the house.

This step conflicts with the ideal of placing the garage and house floor on the same level. Ramps in the confined space of a garage are a nuisance and can sometimes be a hazard unless handrails are also installed. Ramps tend to interfere with maneuvering space for cars and people and make access to vehicles awkward.

An alternative to the step and/or small ramp may be possible by sloping the entire garage floor from the vehicle entrance door up to the house floor level. This continuously sloping floor provides a more uniform and gently sloping surface and will prevent fumes from entering the house. It is advisable to check this solution with local code officials for acceptance.

**Ramps in Garages Can
Be Awkward and Waste Space**

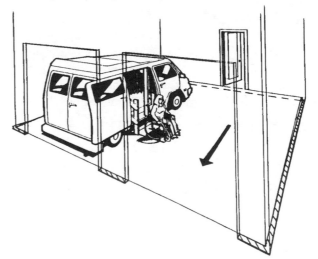

**Sloping Garage Floor Eliminates Need
for Step or Abrupt Ramps for Fume Protection**

Carports and Garages
Changes in Level in Garages

A detached garage connected to the house by a covered open air breezeway will meet all code requirements and provide weather protection. This solution also allows the garage floor, house floor, and connecting accessible routes to be on a common level.

**Garage and House on Same Level
Fume Protection Provided by Open Breezeway**

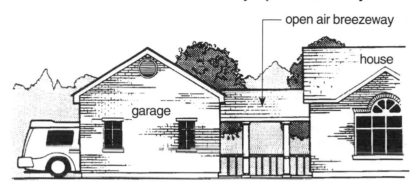

open air breezeway

house

garage

**Building an Extended Roof Out
from the House Also Provides Shelter**

Extended Roof Shelters

Limited shelter can also be provided by including an entry overhang or extended roof from the home that covers the access aisle. The amount of shelter that this overhang provides from rain or snow will depend on how much of the van or car the overhang covers. Use of this type of overhang can be a less expensive and yet still attractive way to emphasize the main entrance to a home.

House with Extended Roof Boarding Shelter

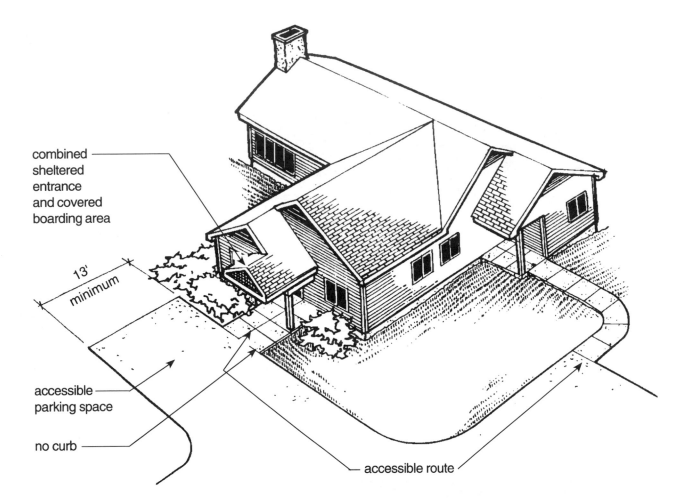

combined
sheltered
entrance
and covered
boarding area

13'
minimum

accessible
parking space

no curb

accessible route

continued on next page

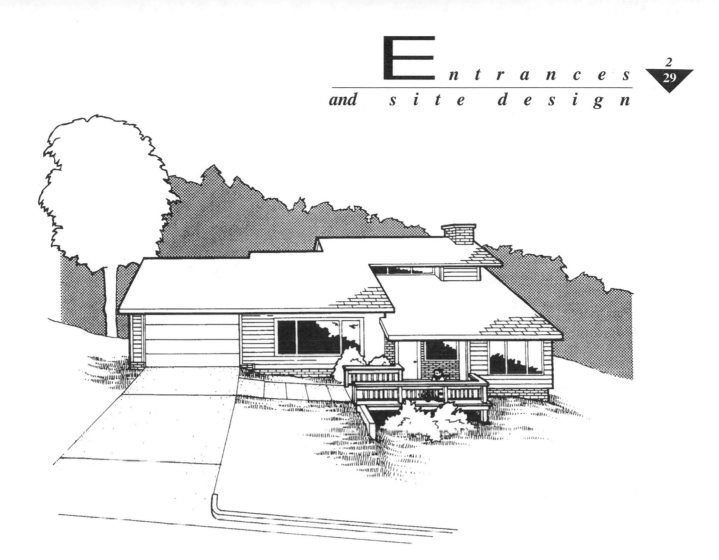

Entrances and Site Design

Accessible entrances and site designs for houses may be radically affected by a complex interplay of technical factors which include: the type and style of the house, natural characteristics of the building site, and the type of construction. House types such as one story, two story or split-level house styles such as traditional, period, or modern; land characteristics which include sloping, flat, wet, or dry; and construction methods such as concrete slab or framed, present interrelated issues for consideration in the design of accessible housing. In addition, there are considerations of cost, safety, image, marketability, aesthetic preferences, and a variety of access features such as ramps and lifts.

In new construction and additions all the factors can be manipulated and controlled to produce attractive yet accessible homes. Conversely, in selecting and modifying an existing house for accessibility, these factors cannot be easily altered. Some innovative design solutions may be all that is needed to create a more universally useable house.

For people who have, or sometime in their lives may acquire, a mobility impairment (or assist a person who has one), a key accessibility issue is eliminating or overcoming steps at entrances and along routes to on-site features or amenities. There are many options to choose from in creating or modifying a house and its site for easy accessibility and each has important consequences. The following material will define and explain the pros and cons of some of these design choices.

Types of Houses and Accessibility
One Story Houses

One story houses are generally ideal for people who have mobility impairments. They eliminate the need for interior stairs or steps, because all living spaces are located on one floor. Because they are, larger in ground area, one story houses require more foundation and roof which makes them more expensive as well as more difficult to place on a site. Single story houses are usually broad and low in appearance. They are not conducive to any "style" of house other than the suburban "ranch-style" house. The single story house may be difficult to find or build in urban areas where land costs are high and lot sizes are small.

One Story Houses

floor level

one story houses are long and low, have large ground area, higher cost, excellent accessibility, and greater safety

Types of Houses and Accessibility

Split-level Houses

Split-level houses are perhaps the most difficult type of house for mobility impaired people. These houses generally have three levels containing major living spaces. The levels are staggered at half story height and connected by short flights of stairs. It is necessary in split-level houses to move from level to level for each activity of daily living. For example, kitchen, dining room, living room, and bedroom space may all be on different levels.

Split-level houses can often be fitted nicely on a sloping site and they do afford greater flexibility in design style than does the single story house. Unfortunately, their interior circulation patterns make them a poor choice for mobility impaired people. Lifts and elevators often do not work well in split-levels because stair spaces are usually too small for lifts, two lifts are usually required, and an elevator if installed would have to be an expensive double-sided multi-stop model.

Also to be avoided are houses with split-level entrance vestibules where one must always go up or down to get to a living space.

Split-level Houses

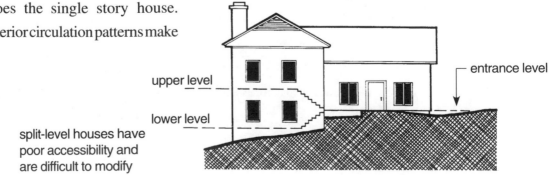

upper level

lower level

entrance level

split-level houses have poor accessibility and are difficult to modify

Types of Houses and Accessibility

Two Story Houses

Because two story houses have smaller ground areas, they require less foundation, roof, and land, which results in lower cost. They are particularly suited for areas where land costs are high. Multi-story houses provide greatest design flexibility for different styles and aesthetics. Multi-story houses are not the best choice for people with mobility impairments. However, if financial and availability factors dictate this type of house, it should have complete accessible living facilities on the floor level that has an accessible entrance. For adequate accessibility, multi-story houses may require installation of a residential elevator or over-the-stair lift. Removable floor areas and ample landings at stairs should be planned into any multi-story house to allow for future addition of either elevators or lifts. Such advanced planning will add little to initial costs and will greatly reduce costs later.

Two Story Houses and Town Houses

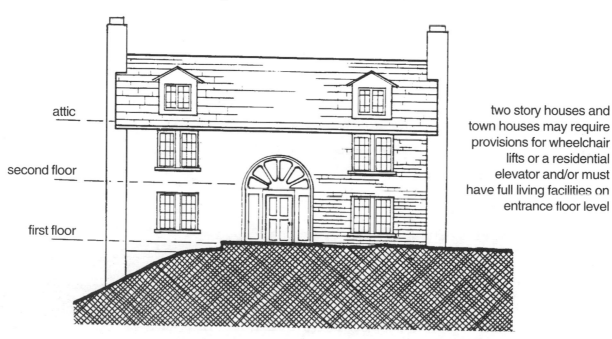

attic

second floor

first floor

two story houses and town houses may require provisions for wheelchair lifts or a residential elevator and/or must have full living facilities on entrance floor level

Construction Types

Slab on Grade Construction

Both framed and slab on grade floor construction methods are commonly used for housing. Slab on grade construction uses concrete for the floor and places the floor level very close to the ground. It is relatively inexpensive, fast, and durable and it makes accessibility quite easy. Its major drawback is the very low profile structure that it produces, almost institutional or commercial in appearance. It is inappropriate in some regions because of extreme climates and does not lend itself to easy alteration.

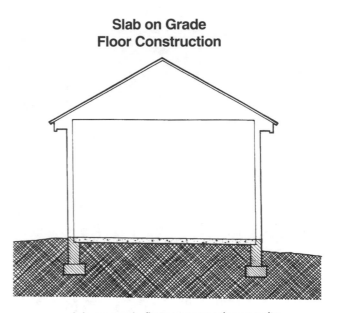

**Slab on Grade
Floor Construction**

slab on grade floor construction results in easy ground level accessibility on flat sites, but produces a low profile image that is not compatible with most popular housing types

Construction Types

Framed Floor Construction

Framed floor construction must be held above the ground to protect it from moisture and insects and to allow air, water, and people to move about below. This type of floor system is probably the most common in housing and whether used over a crawl space, a cellar, or below ground living space, it generally results in a floor level a minimum of 24" to 30" above the nearest outside ground level. It is this change in level from outside to inside the home that must be eliminated or overcome by designing an appropriate accessible entrance.

framed floor systems are popular for their ease of construction and their flexibility for design and future modifications

framed houses require careful placement on the land, use of site planning and selection of access features to create unobtrusive accessible entrances

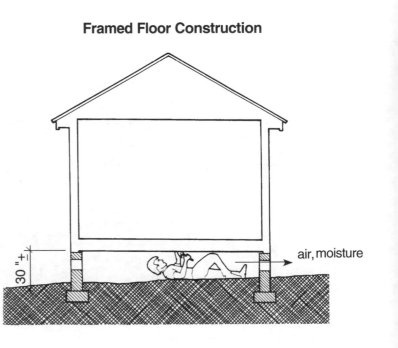

Framed Floor Construction

30 "±

air, moisture

**The Position of the House on
Sloping Land Will Affect Its Accessibility**

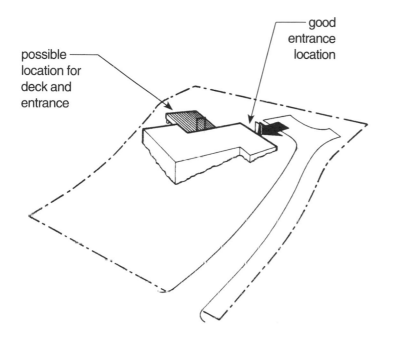

possible location for deck and entrance

good entrance location

House Placement for Entrances

The ideal entrance has a level approach. In new construction, it may be possible to set the the floor level at or close to ground level to eliminate the need for a ramp or limit its length and slope. To some extent, similar techniques can be implemented in modifications using fill dirt and landscaping to modify the terrain.

When installing a framed house on flat land, it may be impossible to bring the floor close to the ground. If the lot has some slope, the uphill side of the house will have the floor closest to the ground and an accessible entrance should be provided at that point. If the property is large enough and zoning permits, the builder may be able to turn the house on the lot or flip the floor plan so the main entrance falls at the most advantageous spot. The most functional solution may be to redesign the proposed floor plan to place an entrance at the best location.

**Rotate, Flip or Redesign Floor Plans to
Place Entrances as Close to Ground as Possible**

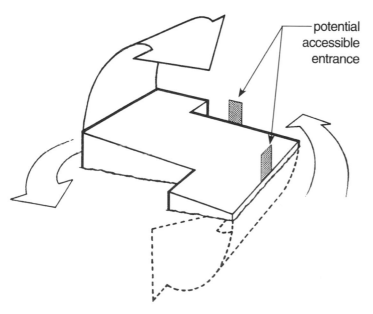

potential accessible entrance

House Placement for Entrances

Earthwork and site grading can be utilized to create attractive accessible entrances. On sloping sites, fill can be added or the land can be cut and graded to place the house floor at ground level. While it is not customary to bring earth to floor levels of framed houses, it can be done successfully if impervious walls, waterproofing, exterior drains, and proper ventilation are provided to keep wood and crawl spaces dry. The waterproofing measures will add cost but the gently sloping accessible entrance will reduce costs because no above ground structure or handrails will be required. With the addition of plantings, such entrances cannot be perceived as special features for accessibility.

Earth Fill at Entrance to Wood Framed House on a Sloping Site

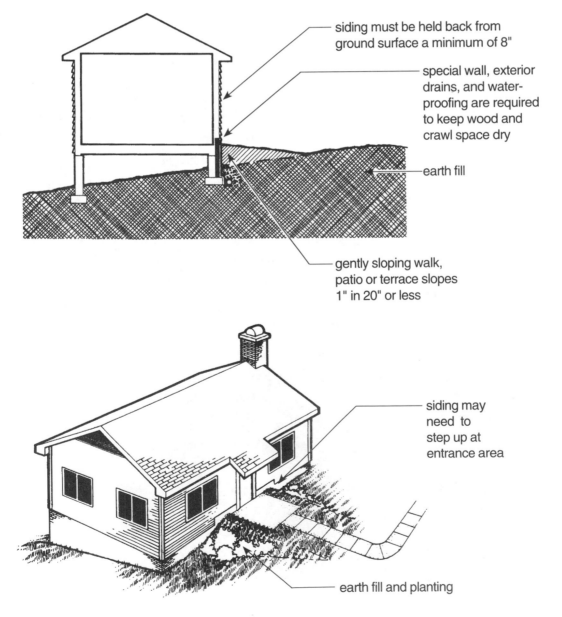

siding must be held back from ground surface a minimum of 8"

special wall, exterior drains, and water- proofing are required to keep wood and crawl space dry

earth fill

gently sloping walk, patio or terrace slopes 1" in 20" or less

siding may need to step up at entrance area

earth fill and planting

Earth Cut Site Grading to Set Wood Framed Floor at Grade on a Sloping Site

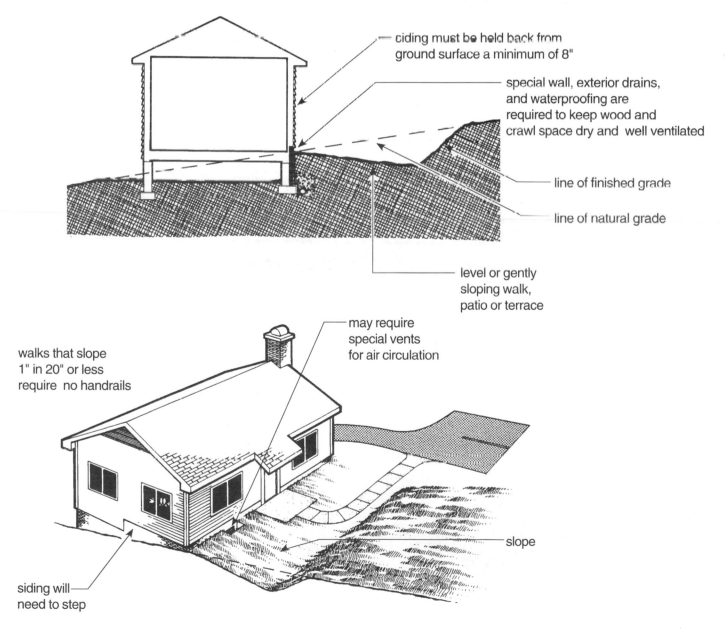

siding must be held back from ground surface a minimum of 8"

special wall, exterior drains, and waterproofing are required to keep wood and crawl space dry and well ventilated

line of finished grade

line of natural grade

level or gently sloping walk, patio or terrace

may require special vents for air circulation

walks that slope 1" in 20" or less require no handrails

slope

siding will need to step

House Placement for Entrances

Short wood framed bridges, spanning from the elevated floor of the house to an uphill site location, create excellent and attractive access elements and eliminate the need for special drainage, waterproofing, and ventilation measures.

On flatter sites, similar bridged entrance solutions are possible by building an earth berm and retaining wall with a sloped walk. There are many advantages to this design. The bridge, since it is level, is not a ramp and may not require handrails (unless local codes stipulate otherwise). Planters, benches, or other features may be used to prevent people from getting too close to an edge. By keeping the sloping walk to a gentle slope of 1" in 20" and flush with the ground, no handrails will be required. The earth berm (artificial hill) and the moat (space between the retaining wall and the house) can be planted with decorative plants so the entire area becomes a terraced garden.

Bridges to Uphill Location on Sloping Sites

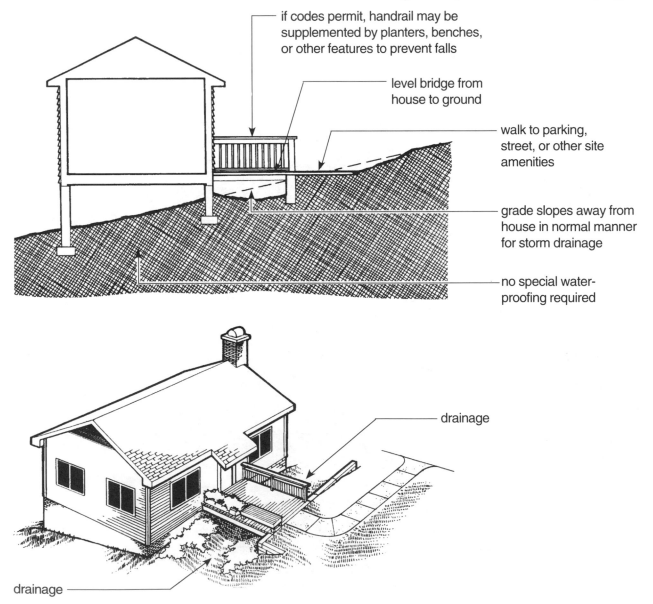

if codes permit, handrail may be supplemented by planters, benches, or other features to prevent falls

level bridge from house to ground

walk to parking, street, or other site amenities

grade slopes away from house in normal manner for storm drainage

no special water-proofing required

drainage

drainage

Bridges to Earth Berms on Flat Sites

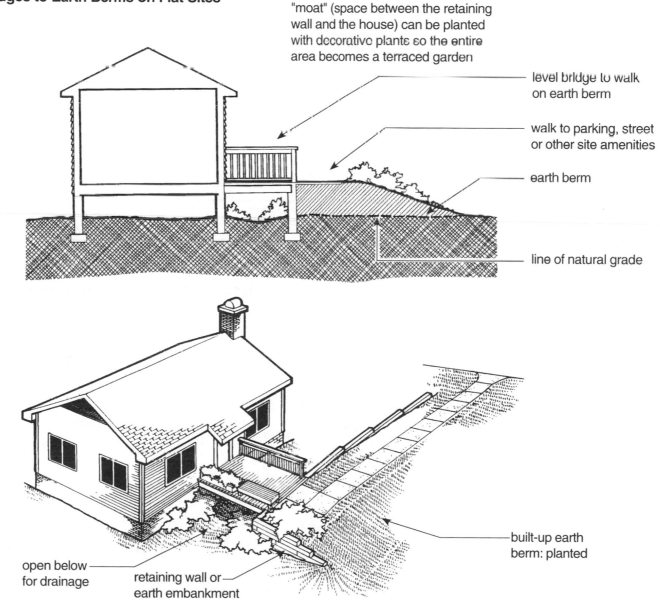

"moat" (space between the retaining wall and the house) can be planted with decorative plants so the entire area becomes a terraced garden

level bridge to walk on earth berm

walk to parking, street or other site amenities

earth berm

line of natural grade

open below for drainage

retaining wall or earth embankment

built-up earth berm: planted

Careful Site Placement and Landscaping Can Eliminate Expensive Construction and Create a More Attractive Installation

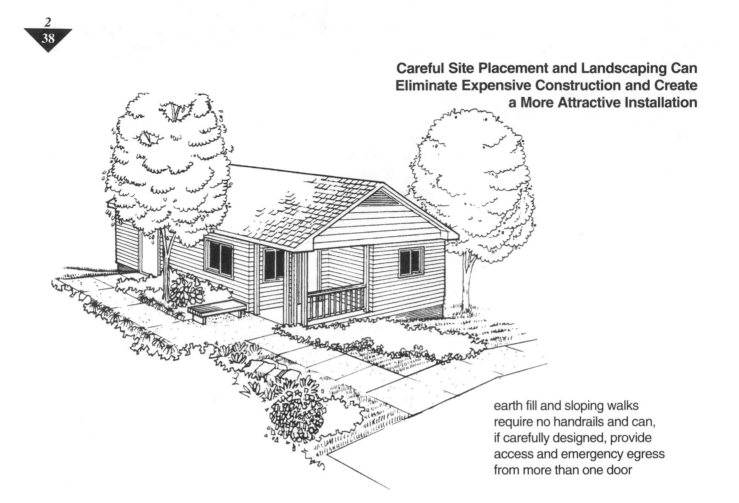

earth fill and sloping walks
require no handrails and can,
if carefully designed, provide
access and emergency egress
from more than one door

Retaining Wall and Earth Fill Installation

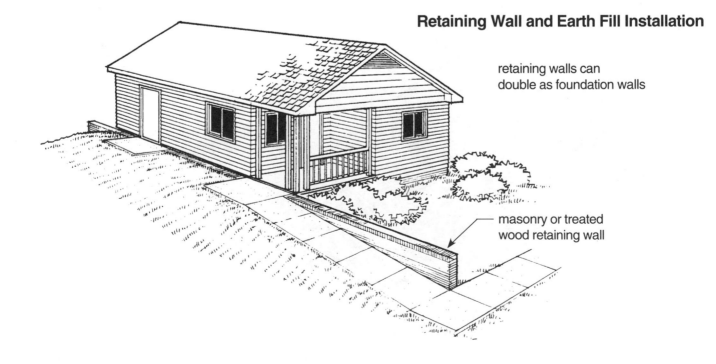

retaining walls can
double as foundation walls

masonry or treated
wood retaining wall

Let the Vehicle Do the Climbing

People generally arrive at buildings via vehicles. There should always be an accessible route from a vehicular parking or drop-off area to at least one accessible entrance. This accessible route may be from a street, bus stop, drop-off zone or parking space. In all cases, and particularly in single family housing, it is best to bring the parking level as close to the floor level of the house as possible to minimize the need for steps, ramps or other level changing devices at the entrance. In other words, let the vehicle do the climbing whenever possible. Careful site planning and house design can make the house fit the site and eliminate changes in level at entrances.

There Should Be an Accessible Route from a Vehicular Parking or Drop-off Area to at Least One Accessible Entrance

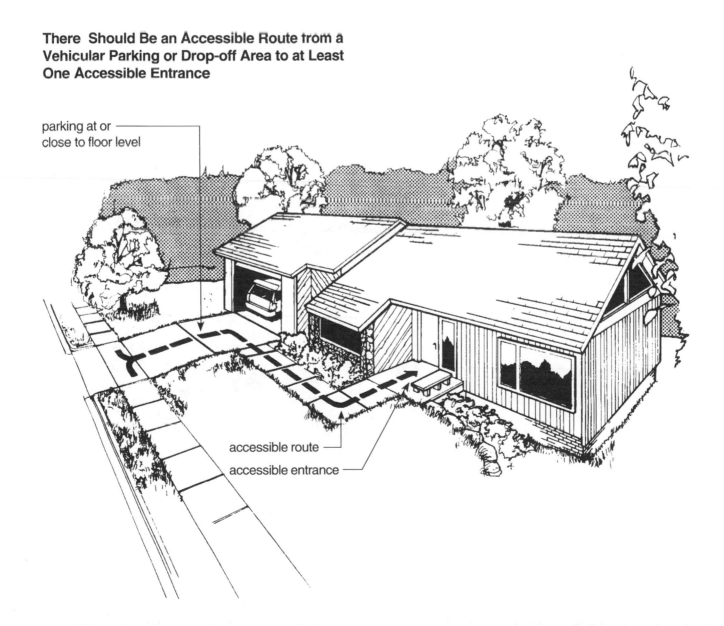

parking at or close to floor level

accessible route

accessible entrance

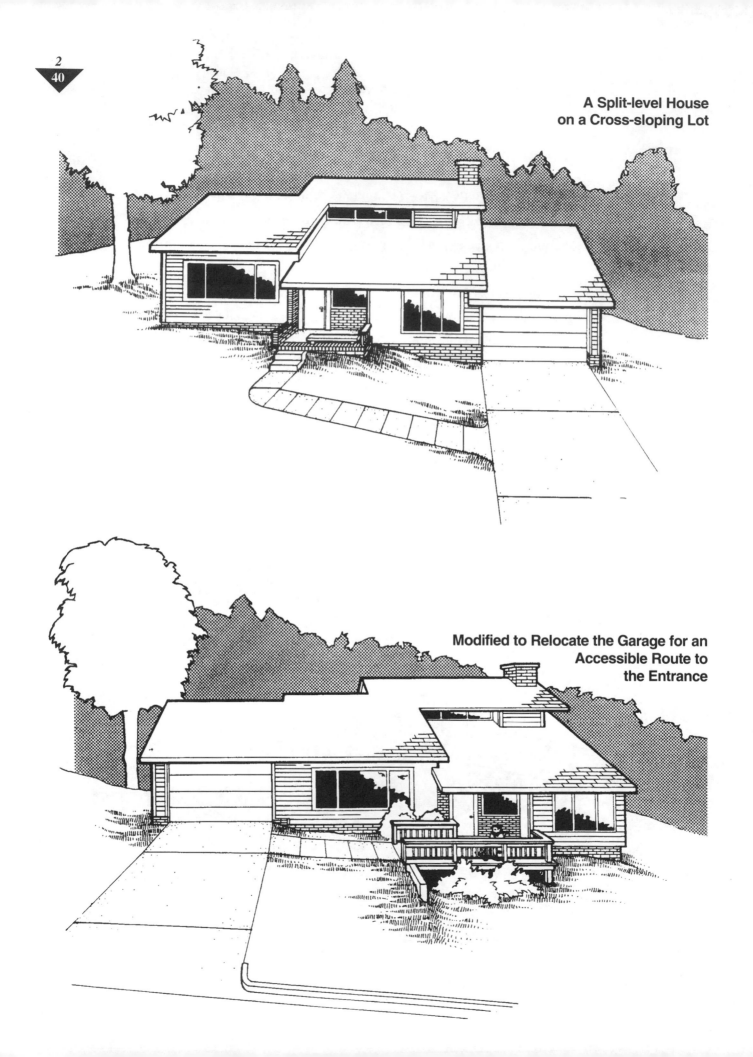

**A Split-level House
on a Cross-sloping Lot**

**Modified to Relocate the Garage for an
Accessible Route to
the Entrance**

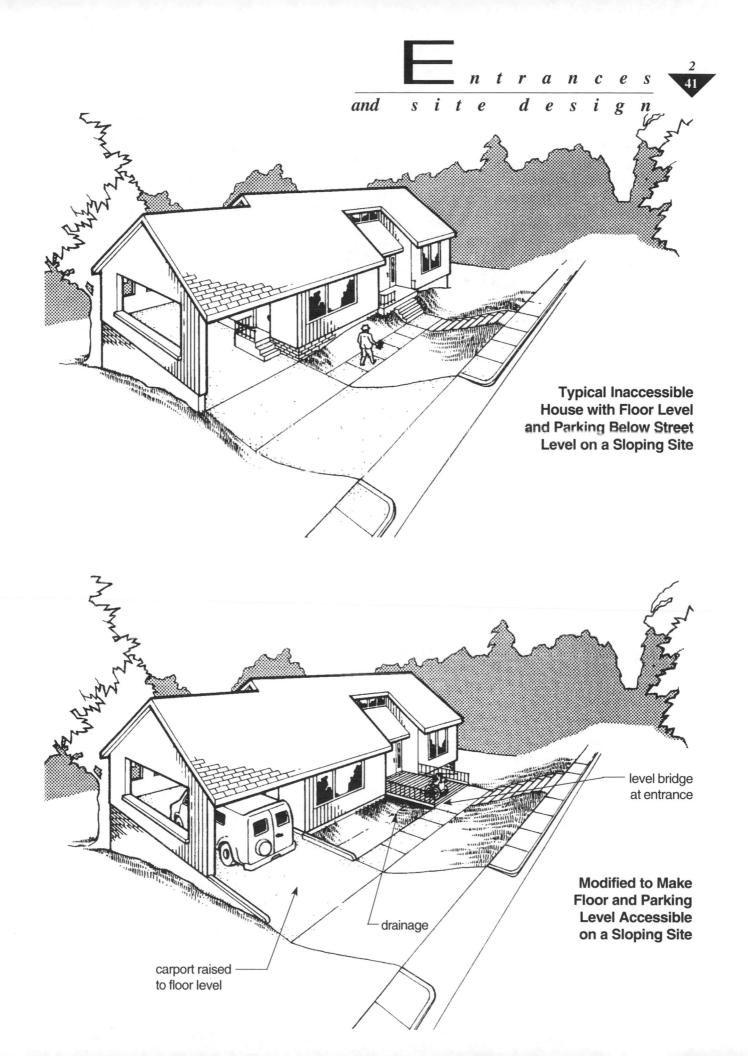

**Typical Inaccessible
House with Floor Level
and Parking Below Street
Level on a Sloping Site**

level bridge
at entrance

**Modified to Make
Floor and Parking
Level Accessible
on a Sloping Site**

drainage

carport raised
to floor level

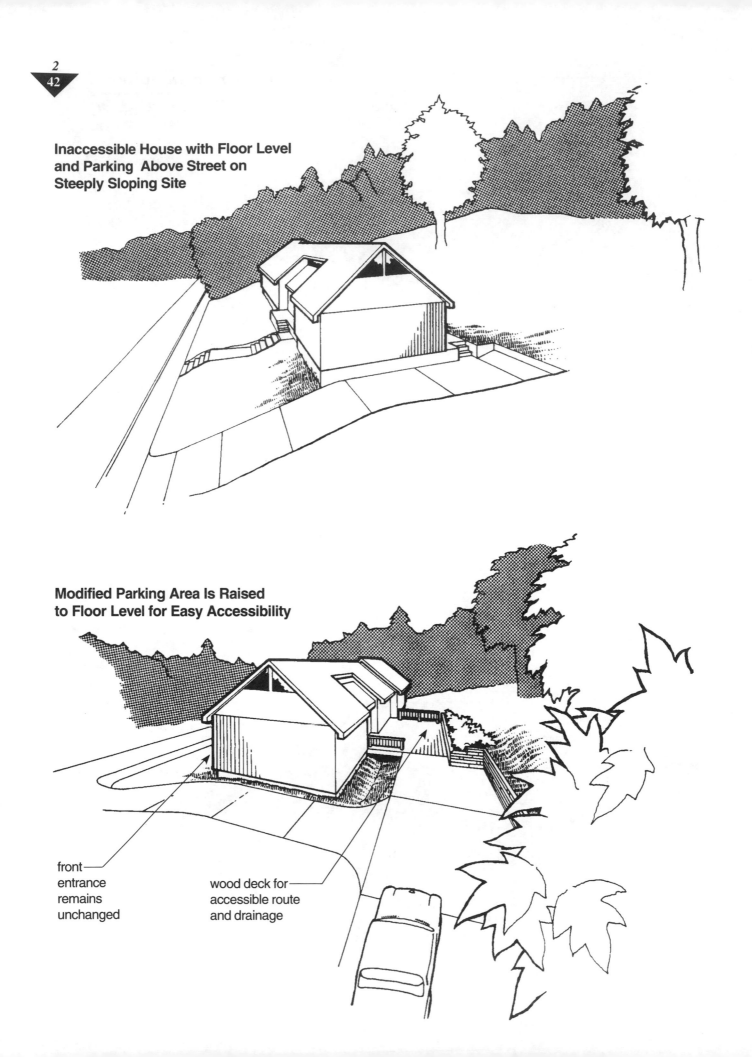

Inaccessible House with Floor Level and Parking Above Street on Steeply Sloping Site

Modified Parking Area Is Raised to Floor Level for Easy Accessibility

front
entrance
remains
unchanged

wood deck for
accessible route
and drainage

Entrance Approach
Sloping Walks

Sloping walks for entrance approaches are gently inclined accessible pathways with shallow slopes that have no drop-off at their edges. They are useful for entrance approaches because they do not require the often out-of-character and expensive handrails that must be installed at steeper sloping ramps. The ANSI and UFAS standards limit sloping walks to a maximum of 1" in 20".

Sloping walks for entrance approaches must have no drop-offs and must meet all the specifications of walks described below. If they have drop-offs or exceed 1" in 20 " in slope, they are considered to be ramps and must meet all ramp requirements.

Note: Walks on residential sites may and often do have drop-offs and exceed these minimum slopes. Such walks cannot be considered accessible routes and additional complying accessible walks should be included.

Entrance Approach
Bridges

Ideal entrance approaches will be level surfaces not requiring ramps or inclined walks. On some sloping sites, level entrance approaches may easily be provided by using bridges to span from the entrance to a retaining wall or the ground on the uphill side of the house. Level bridges provide easy maneuvering space and may have benches, planters, or other elements as edge protection in lieu of handrails.

Entrance Approach

Lifts

Mechanical electrically powered wheelchair lifts can also be used as part of an entrance approach. Several weather resistant lifts are on the market that can be installed outdoors for changes in level at entrances. Such lifts are most useful on existing buildings in urban or densely populated areas where space for ramps and earthwork is not available. Lifts are quite reliable and safe and their only disadvantage is their dependence on electrical power. If the power is interrupted independent access and egress is curtailed. Some lifts do have hand cranks for emergency use but it is time consuming to lower the lift manually.

mechanical weatherproof lift requires electrical service

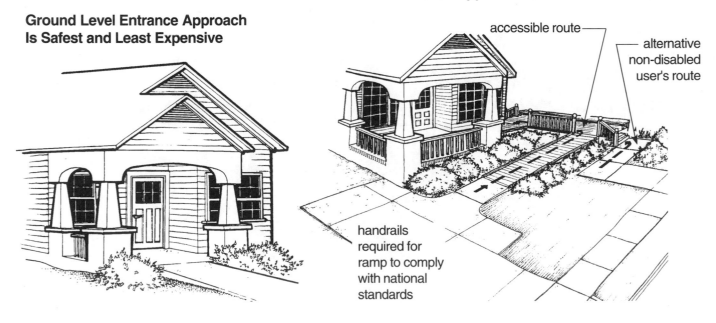

**Varying Combinations of Walks, Steps, Decks, and
Shallow Ramps Can Result in Attractive, Convenient
Entrance Approach for All Users**

**Ground Level Entrance Approach
Is Safest and Least Expensive**

accessible route

alternative non-disabled user's route

handrails required for ramp to comply with national standards

**Ramps at Entrances Can Be an
Obtrusive and Aesthetically Difficult Element**

edge protection
required for ramp
to comply with
national standards

Entrance Approach

Ramps

Ramps are not the only method of providing an entrance approach but they are often necessary because of economy and space limitations. When ramps are planned for new construction, placing the house floor as close as possible to ground level will limit the length and slope of the ramp.

Ramps should be used for entrance approaches where level or sloping walks and bridges or decks are impractical. There are several reasons to avoid using ramps if possible.

Ramps by definition must have handrails and sloping handrails are difficult to incorporate into the design of a house. Ramps thus become very noticeable elements and tend to label a residence as "accessible" or as "a house for people with disabilities".

Ramps can be dangerous for many people who must walk on them. Walking mobility impaired people who use crutches, walkers, or canes and others who have problems walking, may be thrown off balance when using ramps. Whenever possible, steps with proper handrails should be included along with ramps so walking people are not forced to use the ramps.

In ice and snow conditions, ramps are dangerous for everyone. Where climates warrant, snow melting equipment or roofs over ramps should be considered.

**Ramps May Be
Dangerous for Some People**

**Combination Stairs and Ramp at Entrance
Provide Choices for People and Improve Safety**

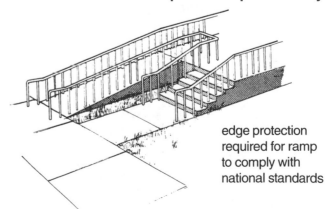

edge protection
required for ramp
to comply with
national standards

Entrance Approach

Ramp Characteristics

An accessible route or pathway that slopes more than 1" in 20" is considered to be a ramp by the ANSI and UFAS standards and must meet the following requirements:

Entrance Approach

Ramp Slope

The maximum slope of a ramp should be the ratio of 1 in 12. For example, a ramp installed to provide access to a floor level 18" above the ground would need to be at least 18' long. Difficulty in using ramps and the chance of accidents on ramps increases with the slope. As a result, ramps with slopes less than the maximum 1" in 12" are safer and recommended whenever possible.

Entrance Approach

Ramp Width

The minimum clear width for ramps is 3'-0" according to the ANSI and UFAS standards. 3'-0" is extremely narrow and requires precise control of wheelchairs on a sloping surface which is difficult for some people to manage. 4'-0" is recommended as a minimum clear width to allow more maneuvering space. A 4'-0" width will allow one wheelchair user and one walking person to pass. 5'-0" clear width will permit easier two-way traffic.

Minimum Ramp Widths

3'- 0" minimum for one-way traffic
4'- 0" recommended
5'- 0" minimum for two-way traffic

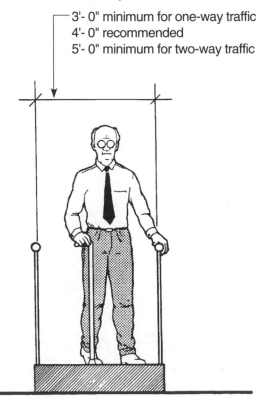

**The Maximum Ramp Slope
Is Too Steep for Some People**

Entrance Approach
Ramp Length

The maximum length of a single ramp segment between level platforms is 30' for steeper slopes (1 in 16 to the maximum slope of 1 in 12), and 40' for lesser slopes (1 in 20 to 1 in 16). Length of ramp segments is limited because many people do not have the stamina to climb longer distances and need a level area to rest. Subtle differences in the definitions of sloping walks and ramps occur between UFAS and ANSI.

**Maximum Length of a
UFAS Complying Ramp**

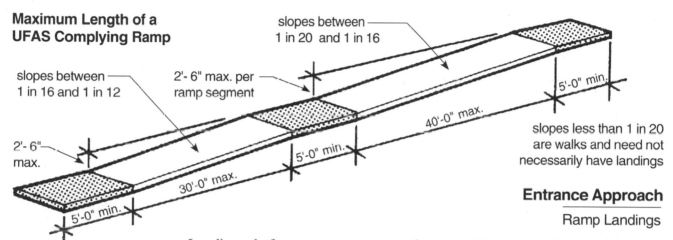

slopes between
1 in 20 and 1 in 16

slopes between
1 in 16 and 1 in 12

2'- 6" max. per
ramp segment

2'- 6"
max.

40'-0" max.

5'-0" min.

slopes less than 1 in 20
are walks and need not
necessarily have landings

5'-0" min.

30'-0" max.

5'-0" min.

Entrance Approach
Ramp Landings

Landing platforms are necessary at the top and bottom of all ramp segments. The platforms are required by the ANSI and UFAS standards to be at least 5'-0" long by the width of the ramp. If ramps change direction, the platform must be at least 5'-0" by 5'-0". Platforms must be level except for a minimum slope to allow water to run off. Landing platforms at doors should be larger than 5'-0" by 5'-0" to allow ample maneuvering space at the door.

**Minimum Platform Size
at Change of Direction**

**Larger Platforms Preferred at Doors
(see "Maneuvering Space at Doors"
and "Entrance Platforms")**

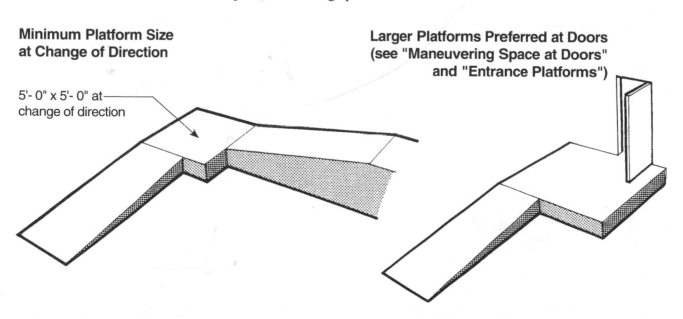

5'- 0" x 5'- 0" at
change of direction

Entrance Approach

Cross Slope

There can be no cross slope on ramps greater than approximately 3/16" per 1'.

Entrance Approach

Ramp Handrails

Ramps that rise more than 6"or are longer than 6'- 0" are required by UFAS and ANSI standards to have handrails on both sides. Among the specifications for the handrails are the following key features:

1. Top surface of handrail at 30" to 34" above the floor or ground.

2. Handrails extend at least 1'- 0" beyond the top and bottom of the ramp and run parallel to the floor or the ground below.

3. Handrail has continuous surface shaped for easy gripping.

4. For wall-mounted rails, the space between the handrail and the wall is exactly 1-1/2".

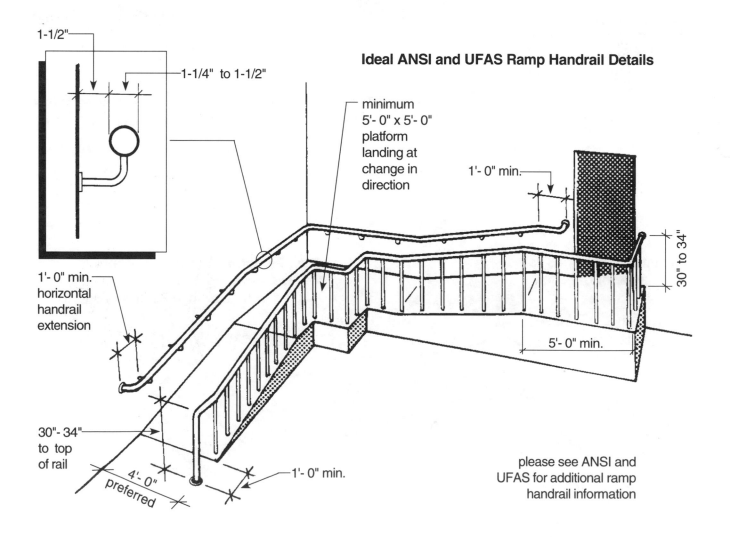

Ideal ANSI and UFAS Ramp Handrail Details

1-1/2"

1-1/4" to 1-1/2"

minimum 5'- 0" x 5'- 0" platform landing at change in direction

1'- 0" min.

30" to 34"

1'- 0" min. horizontal handrail extension

5'- 0" min.

30"- 34" to top of rail

4'- 0" preferred

1'- 0" min.

please see ANSI and UFAS for additional ramp handrail information

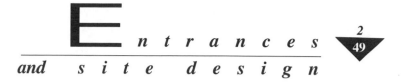

Handrail Shapes

1-1/4" to 1-1/2"

round

oval

shaped

1-1/2"

3/4" ±

1" ±

1-1/2"   1-1/2"

Entrance Approach

Handrail Size and Shape

Handrails must be "gripable". 1-1/4" to 1-1/2" diameter pipe railings work well and oval shapes of similar circumference are acceptable. Railings can also be shaped in solid wood or other materials.

Wheelchairs, Crutches, Canes, and Strollers Can Pass Under Handrails

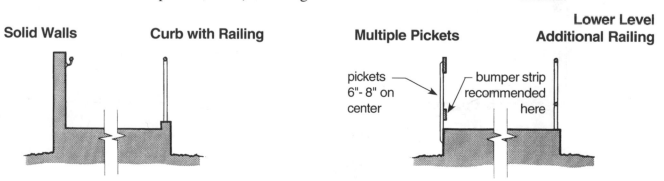

Entrance Approach

Edge Protection at Ramps

Edge protection is provided because handrails alone may not be sufficient to prevent someone from falling over the edge of ramps and landings that have drop-offs. Edges might be protected by: 1) installing solid walls with wall mounted handrails, 2) adding a curb along the edge, 3) using multiple closely spaced handrail pickets, and 4) including a lower horizontal rail below the handrail.

Solid Walls   **Curb with Railing**   **Multiple Pickets**   **Lower Level Additional Railing**

pickets 6"- 8" on center

bumper strip recommended here

Entrance Approach

Alternate Ramp Designs

Ramps with sloping handrails and/or edge protection features can be obtrusive elements that are difficult to include into the design of a house in an appealing manner . The information on ramps described thus far is compatible with ANSI and UFAS standards. However, not all housing will have to meet these standards, especially single family residences and small privately owned housing. Not everyone needs handrails on both sides of their ramps– a power wheelchair user, for example, would never use such handrails. Therefore, unless local codes require them, some owners and builders may wish to omit or modify some ramp features or use alternate edge protection elements in the design of their houses.

Curbs with no handrails may be adequate edge protection, for very wide, shallow ramps. Other alternative edge protection elements may include plant boxes or benches and shelves for packages or potted plants in lieu of handrails. Such elements are common on decks and porches and may work well for some gently sloping ramps and for level bridges.

Handrails Are Required at Most Ramps and Are a Good Edge Protector at Any Drop-off

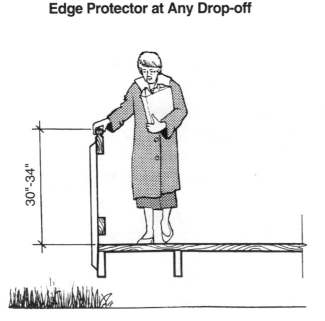

30"-34"

Planters and Benches As Edge Protectors

wide planters or benches can be an attractive way to keep people away from drop-offs on decks, bridges, and very shallow ramps

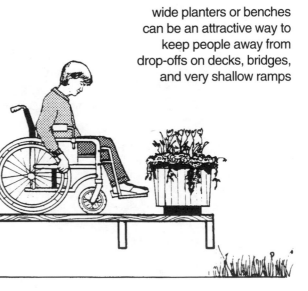

Entrance Approach
Ramp Configurations

Ramp segments should be straight runs whenever possible. Ramps can turn corners, switch back or be arranged in any form so long as a minimum 5'-0" by 5'-0" landing is provided whenever they change direction. Curved ramps should be avoided because they create severe cross slopes. However, curved ramps of very large radius may be acceptable if their cross slope does not exceed 1 in 50 or 3/16" per foot.

Entrance Approach
Ramp Materials

Ramps can be constructed of any weatherproof material. Concrete, brick, and pressure preservative treated wood are common. Surfaces should be textured to be as non-slip as possible. Carborundum grit adhesive strips can be used on some ramps to create a non-slip surface texture. All ramp surfaces get wet and can develop moss or fungus growth that is extremely slippery, requiring periodic cleaning or maintenance. Treated wood ramps, properly ventilated, can be expected to last for 10 to 15 years.

Entrance Approach
Portable Ramps

In situations requiring temporary accessibility, such as existing rental housing where permanent modifications are not appropriate for entrance approach, a portable ramp system may be a good alternative. There are portable ramp systems available that can be assembled from manufactured components to create access ramps. The manufactured ramp systems can be disassembled and moved to a new location–an advantage for the disabled individual who may move frequently. One disadvantage of portable ramp systems is their metal fabrication which is not compatible with house construction and makes the ramps quite noticeable. Decorative planting can help to conceal these unattractive but functional ramps.

Prefabricated Metal Ramp System

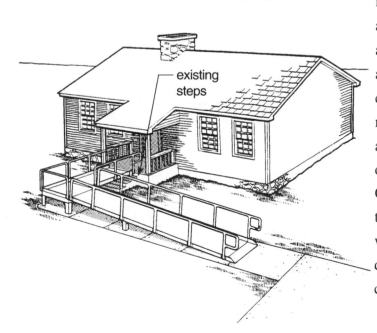

existing steps

Entrances

Characteristics of Accessible Entrances

An entrance is made up of several components: 1) the actual door, 2) the interior and exterior floor/ ground area in the immediate proximity of the door, 3) the surrounding structure of the building, and 4) the segment of the accessible pedestrian route used for entrance approach. Each of these components have detailed features or characteristics that can affect the accessibility of the entrance.

There are essential features that must be a part of every accessible entrance and important options that improve usability for everyone. Described below are some characteristics of accessible entrances.

Essential Features	Purpose
Level clear floor space both inside and out ▲ Size of floor space will vary depending on the door configuration (see "Doors") ▲ Floor space may slope to allow water to run off (see "Maneuvering Space at Entrance Doors ")	To provide maneuvering space at doors
Flush or low threshold ▲ Maximum of 1/4" vertical change in level (see "Thresholds")	To eliminate obstacles to wheels and any tripping hazards
Wide door ▲ At least 36" in width	To provide ample open clearance for passage and comply with minimum 32" clear opening specified in the standards
Force to open door ▲ No more than 5 lbs. of pressure preferred ▲ Maximum of 8.5 lbs.	To allow operation by people with limited strength
Easily operated latch ▲ Lever handles preferred (see "Hardware at Entrance Doors")	To be activated without requiring gripping, twisting, or more than 5 lbs. of force, a benefit to people with limited use of their hands

Important Optional Features	Purpose
Shelter ▲ Covered entrances	To provide weather protection while unlocking the door, greeting a caller, etc.
Package shelf ▲ 10"- 12" wide minimum recommended at table or railing height	To provide space for packages while unlocking and opening the door. Eliminates trips, bending, stooping down, and requirement to balance parcels
Peephole, sidelights, or viewing windows in entrance doors ▲ Placed so that short , seated, or standing people can see who is at the door	To improve security
Lighting ▲ Moderate level of general illumination outside the door ▲ Lighted door bell button ▲ Concentrated light on the lockset	To allow residents to see callers and to help low vision users find and operate the bell and lock
Push panel ▲ A smooth 12"- 16" high full width panel mounted near the bottom push side of the door (see "Push Panel")	To provide a smooth durable pushing surface for wheelchair bumpers and to protect the door from damage
Auxiliary handles ▲ Second handle on the pull side of the door near the hinge edge (see "Auxiliary Handle")	To provide a method for mobility impaired people to pull the door closed after passing through the doorway
Power door operator ▲ Special motor driven device that opens and closes a door with the press of a switch (see "Power Operators")	To provide independent use of the door by people who are unable to open doors

Features of an Accessible Entrance at a Small Porch

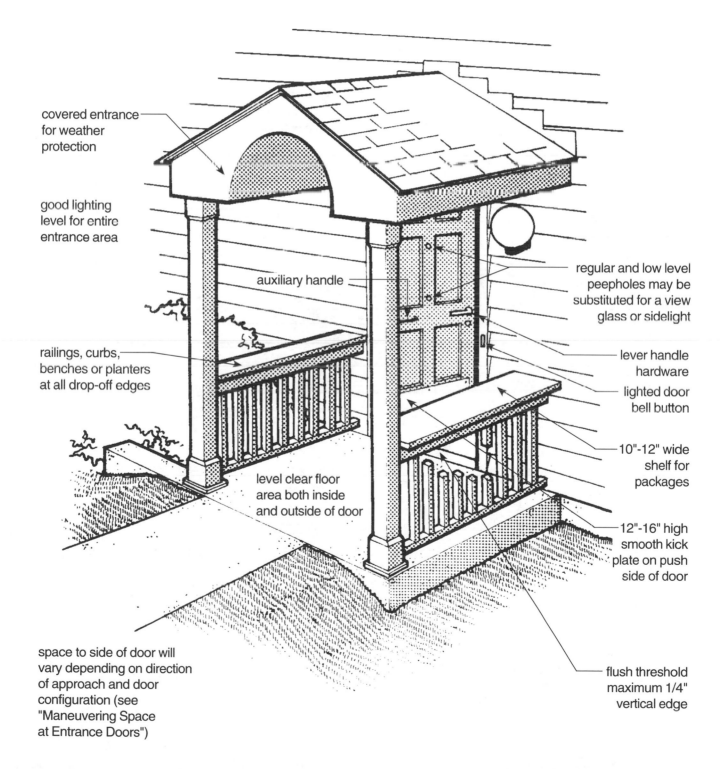

covered entrance for weather protection

good lighting level for entire entrance area

auxiliary handle

railings, curbs, benches or planters at all drop-off edges

level clear floor area both inside and outside of door

regular and low level peepholes may be substituted for a view glass or sidelight

lever handle hardware

lighted door bell button

10"-12" wide shelf for packages

12"-16" high smooth kick plate on push side of door

flush threshold maximum 1/4" vertical edge

space to side of door will vary depending on direction of approach and door configuration (see "Maneuvering Space at Entrance Doors")

Features of an Accessible Entrance at a Large Porch

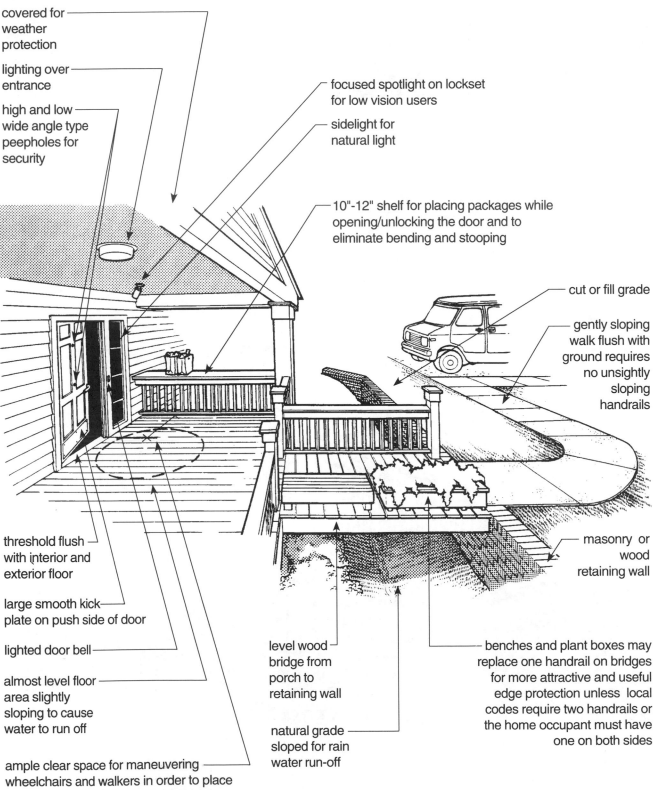

covered for weather protection

lighting over entrance

high and low wide angle type peepholes for security

focused spotlight on lockset for low vision users

sidelight for natural light

10"-12" shelf for placing packages while opening/unlocking the door and to eliminate bending and stooping

cut or fill grade

gently sloping walk flush with ground requires no unsightly sloping handrails

threshold flush with interior and exterior floor

large smooth kick plate on push side of door

lighted door bell

almost level floor area slightly sloping to cause water to run off

masonry or wood retaining wall

level wood bridge from porch to retaining wall

natural grade sloped for rain water run-off

benches and plant boxes may replace one handrail on bridges for more attractive and useful edge protection unless local codes require two handrails or the home occupant must have one on both sides

ample clear space for maneuvering wheelchairs and walkers in order to place packages on shelf, to approach and open door, and for conversations with callers - minimum 6' x 8' suggested

Entrances
Screen and Storm Doors

Many people with disabilities have great difficulty using a single door. Screen and storm doors further complicate entrance use for most people with mobility impairments and it is best to avoid having such doors. However, where screen or storm doors are necessary, they are best installed with auxiliary handles and no automatic closer or springs for closing. Thus equipped, the doors can be left standing open while one passes through and then pulled closed from the inside.

Entrances
Maneuvering Space at Entrance Doors

Clear level floor space is needed on both the inside and the outside of entrance doors. On the outside, the space can slope slightly to cause the water to run off. A maximum slope of 1 in 50 or 3/16" per foot should suffice. The maneuvering space varies in size depending upon many factors including the direction of approach and the swing of the door.

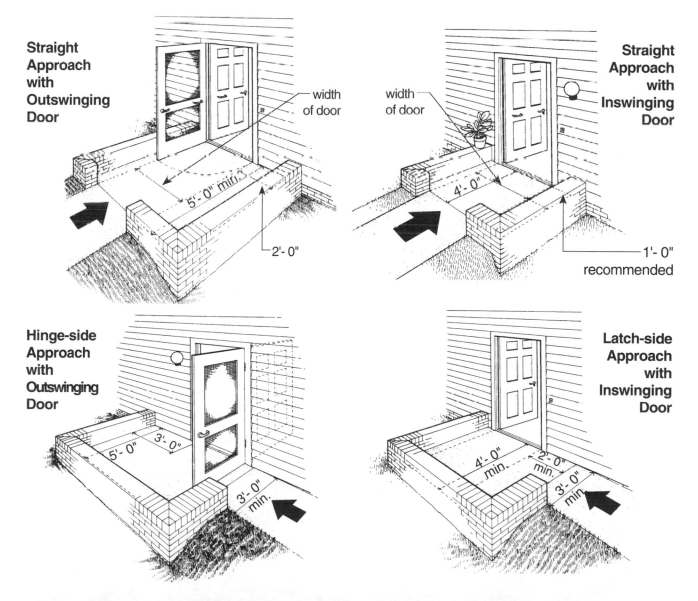

Straight Approach with Outswinging Door

width of door

5'-0" min.

2'-0"

Straight Approach with Inswinging Door

width of door

4'-0"

1'-0" recommended

Hinge-side Approach with Outswinging Door

5'-0"   3'-0"

3'-0" min.

Latch-side Approach with Inswinging Door

4'-0" min.   2'-0" min.

3'-0" min.

Entrances

Hardware at Entrance Doors

The following items/hardware are recommended at accessible entrance doors. Please see characteristics of accessible entrances above and the section on "Doors" for additional information on entrance doors and other types of doors.

Entrances

Thresholds

The floor inside and the platform outside each door should be at the same level. All thresholds should be as flat as possible and have no vertical change in level greater than 1/4", or 1/2" if the threshold is beveled at 45 degrees.

In new construction, threshold problems can be eliminated by setting the door sill onto the subfloor so the finished flooring is flush with or nearly flush with the top of the sill. To avoid water problems, stop flashing should be used and a 1/4" gap can be added between the outside floor surface and the door sill. The gap will allow water to drain away without contacting the door sill.

Acceptable Threshold

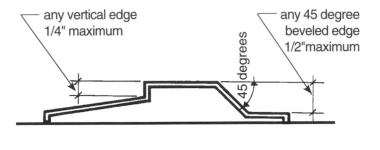

Dropped Sill at Exterior Door

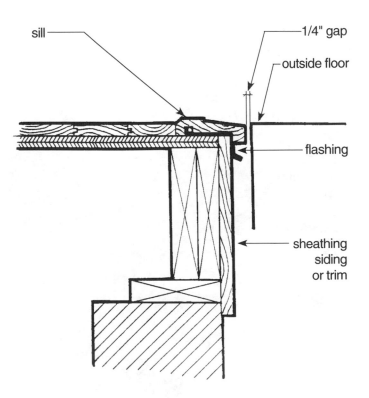

Entrances

Door Handles and Latches

Many people who have limited use of their hands have difficulty using standard smooth round door knobs. Lever handles, push plates, and push bars are usable by almost everyone. At entrance doors, people frequently have their hands full with packages while using keys to unlock the door. Lever handles provide a welcome alternative. They are readily available in all price ranges and are highly recommended for all entrance doors including screen and storm doors.

**Round Knobs Are
Difficult for Most People**

**Lever Handles Can Be
Operated Easily by Everyone**

Entrances

Door Locks

Many people with limited hand use have difficulty grasping and using keys required for entrance locks. Often keys can be adapted by attaching them to a larger handle or strap that makes the key easier to grasp. For some people, a push button combination lock or an electronic lock that uses a plastic "credit card" key may be a better choice.

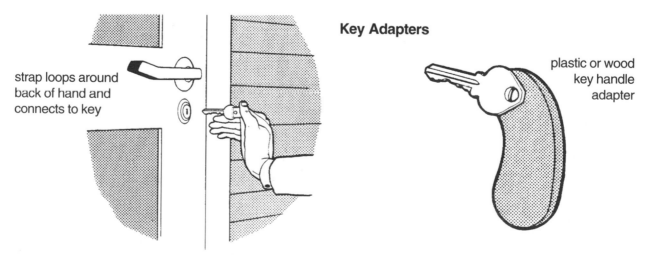

strap loops around
back of hand and
connects to key

Key Adapters

plastic or wood
key handle
adapter

Entrances
Push Panels

Doors with stiles or raised panels close to the floor will be damaged by wheelchairs being used to push them open. Screen and glass doors can be broken by the front bumpers or front foot rests on the chairs. Door stiles and raised panels snag on chairs and make passage difficult. It is best if a smooth full width panel is provided at the bottom of all entrance doors. The smooth panel should be at least 12"-16" high and located on the push side. Metal, plastic, and acrylic kick panels can be installed to match the decor of the surrounding hardware and fixtures.

Push Panel

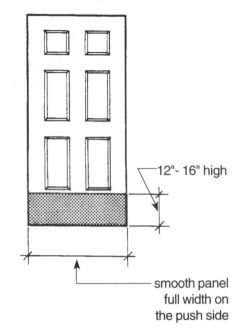

12"- 16" high

smooth panel
full width on
the push side

Entrances

Auxiliary Handles

Mobility impaired people who use walkers, wheelchairs, crutches, and braces have difficulty reaching the door handle to pull it closed. A small loop-type handle mounted 6" to 8" from the hinge edge and 36" maximum above the floor, on the pull side of the door, will help alleviate this problem.

Auxiliary Handles

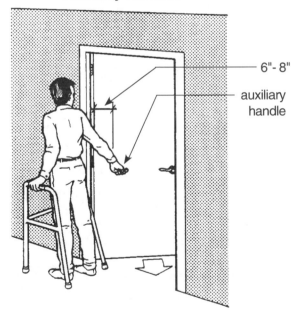

6"- 8"

auxiliary
handle

Entrances

Weather Stripping and Closers

Weather stripping and automatic closers are common on entrance doors and both can make doors more difficult to open. Some people cannot use an entrance door that requires more than 5-8 pounds of force to open. If doors exceed this limit, weather stripping may need to be altered, or a closer or spring may need to be omitted and replaced with an auxiliary handle for closing. If neither of these suggestions is practical, a power door operator may provide a viable option (see "Power Door Operators" below).

Entrances

Power Operators for Entrance Doors

Small, light-duty, power door operators for residential doors are available from several manufacturers. These motor driven operators are similar to the larger and more expensive commercial versions seen at store and airport entrances.

The operator mounts onto the top of the door and opens and closes the door when activated by a switch. Several types of switches are available including touch pads that can be wall or post mounted, electronic infrared and radio switches which turn on when movement is detected or when a hand held transmitter is activated, and pressure switches which are activated when weight is placed on a floor panel or strip. Once the door is opened, it stays open for a preset amount of time, or until another switch is activated to close the door.

Equipped with an electronic latch and lock, the power operator makes door operation fully automatic for people who have difficulty using locks and doors. Power door operators are also an alternative in renovations when an inadequate amount of maneuvering space is available for wheelchair and walker users.

Door operators also permit manual operation so that if the power fails the door can still be opened or closed. Manual operation permits other family members to use the door without operating the power unit. Light-duty, low-energy, slow moving power door openers can be added to existing doors or built-in as part of new construction. When added to existing doors, the device and the wiring is sometimes exposed above the door. In new construction, it is possible to conceal most of the opener behind wood work or an appearance panel.

Power Door Operators Are Useful for People Who Cannot Manage Manual Doors and Where Maneuvering Space is Inadequate

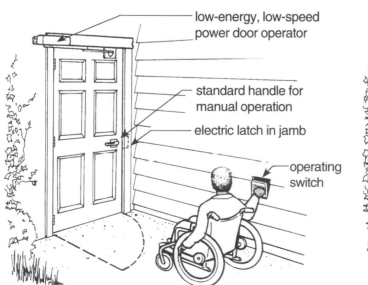

low-energy, low-speed power door operator

standard handle for manual operation

electric latch in jamb

operating switch

PUSH

Package Shelves

Entrances

Package Shelves at Entrance Doors

A shelf or other surface near an entrance door where one unlocks and opens the door is a good feature for everyone. It eliminates extra trips, bending over, or difficult balancing of parcels while operating locks. A low wall or wide railing can suffice if the top is at least 10"-12" wide and 30"-34" above the floor.

wall or railing with a wide top

Walks

Walks are a vital part of the accessible route that is necessary for people to get to and from the house, parking, site amenities, bus stops, and other buildings on the site. There are features of walks that affect their usability and safety for people with different types of disabilities. Following is a brief description of these characteristics and their effect on users.

Note: Not all walks must or can have all of the following characteristics but only those that do are considered to be an accessible route as defined by the ANSI and UFAS Standards. There may be two or more routes for getting from one point to another on a site– only one need be an accessible route.

Walks
Width

Walks for one-way passage by wheelchair users must be at least 3'- 0" wide.

Walks to accommodate one wheelchair and one walking person in passing or side by side must be at least 4'- 0" wide.

Walks to allow two wheelchairs to pass must be at least 5'- 0" wide.

One-way Passage

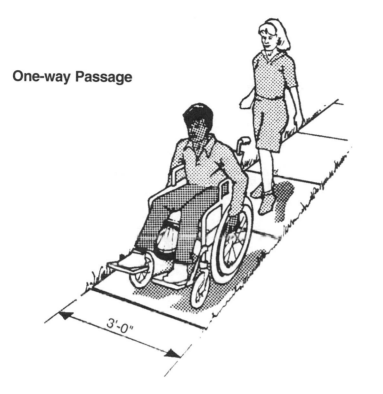

3'-0"

Wheelchair and Walking Passage

4'-0"

Two-way Wheelchair Passage

5'-0"

Walks
Width

Walks should be wide throughout their length
or widened at site features such as telephones,
benches, and water fountains.

Passing Spaces

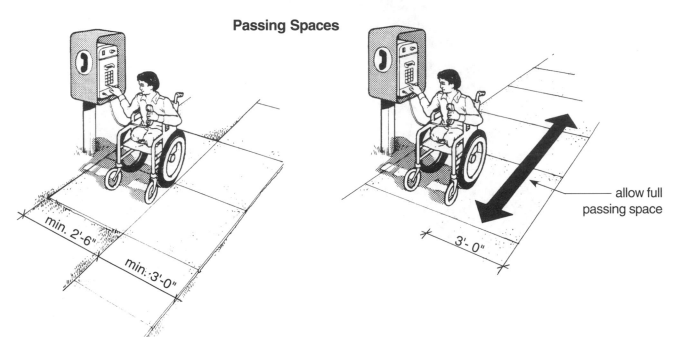

min. 2'-6"

min. 3'-0"

3'-0"

allow full
passing space

Where very long and narrow walks are used, passing
and rest spaces should be provided at intervals. Passing
spaces should be at least 5'-6" x 6'-0".

Passing Spaces Along Narrow Walks

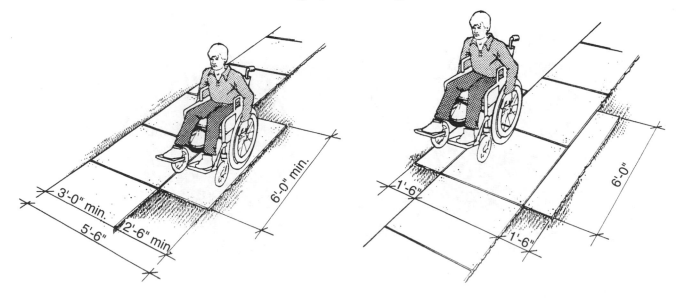

3'-0" min.

6'-0" min.

5'-6"   2'-6" min.

1'-6"

6'-0"

1'-6"

Walks
Surface

Walk surfaces must be firm and capable of supporting concentrated loads such as those caused by crutch tips, narrow wheels, and canes. Paving materials, compacted stone, and some organic ground covers such as pine straw may be acceptable. Loose gravel, sand, and plant material such as grass are not acceptable surfaces. These surfaces are too difficult for wheelchair users to push through and they contribute to slipping and tripping accidents for people who have difficulty walking.

**Loose Sand or
Grass Is Not Acceptable**

Detectable Shoreline

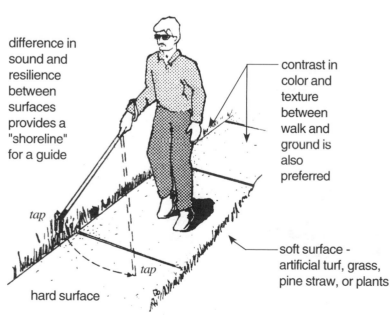

difference in sound and resilience between surfaces provides a "shoreline" for a guide

tap

tap

hard surface

contrast in color and texture between walk and ground is also preferred

soft surface - artificial turf, grass, pine straw, or plants

Walk surfaces that differ significantly from the adjacent materials are best for people with low vision or blindness. The difference in resilience between a concrete walk and grass beside the walk provides a guiding "shoreline" for blind people. The sound and feel of the dissimilar surfaces, detected by tapping with a cane, helps to guide the blind pedestrian. The contrast in color or reflectivity is a benefit to low vision people.

Walks

Changes in Level

Walk surfaces must have no abrupt change in level greater than
1/4". Surfaces of walks must be kept free of debris such as stones,
nuts, and twigs that can jamb wheelchair wheels and twist ankles.
It may be best to place walks away from trees that drop fruit.

**Walk Surfaces Must Have No Abrupt
Change in Level and Must Be Kept Free of Debris**

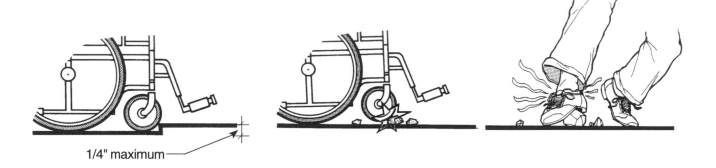

1/4" maximum

Walks

Drop-offs

Any drop-off at the edge of walks is a hazard for wheelchair
users. A change in level of as little as 1-1/2" to 2" can throw a person
off balance and cause a fall. If significant drop-offs are unavoidable,
edge protection similar to that required for ramps may be needed.

**Unexpected Drop-offs At Edges of Walks and
Unprotected Edges at Ramps and Stoops Can Be Hazardous**

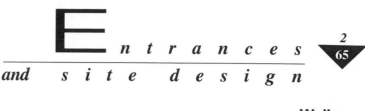
Walks
Slope

Accessible walks can slope up to 1 in 20. Paths which are steeper than 1 in 20 and part of an accessible route, are considered to be ramps by the ANSI and UFAS standards and by definition must have handrails and edge protection (see "Ramps").

Note: Not all walks must be accessible routes and not all locations require ANSI/UFAS compliance. Therefore, some walks may be steeper than the allowable 1 in 20 and not have handrails.

Handrails at Walks

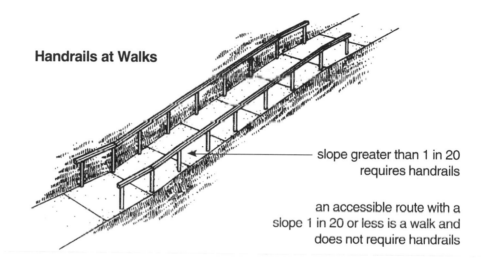

slope greater than 1 in 20 requires handrails

an accessible route with a slope 1 in 20 or less is a walk and does not require handrails

Accessible Walks Have Little or No Cross Slope

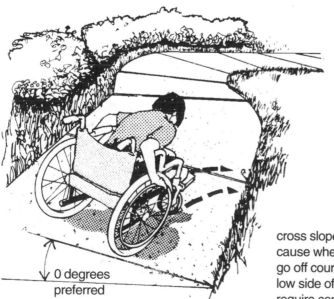

0 degrees preferred

Walks
Cross Slope

There should be little or no cross slope on accessible walks. Steep cross slopes tend to pull people off balance and cause wheelchairs to go off course.

cross slope on walks cause wheelchairs to go off course toward the low side of the walk and require constant correction

Walks

Headroom

Clear headroom, free of overhanging limbs or other elements, should be maintained to a height of at least 6'-8" above accessible walks. People who are blind or have low vision may not be able to detect and avoid overhanging elements or protruding objects that extend over the walks.

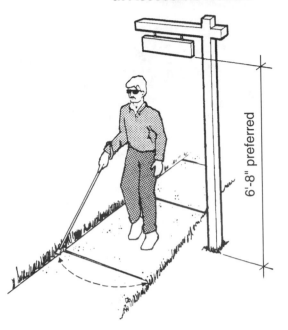

Overhanging Objects at Accessible Routes

6'-8" preferred

Walks

Crossings at Driveways

When walks cross driveways or streets their surface must blend to the same level as the vehicular surface with no abrupt change in level greater than 1/4".

Where cobblestones or other heavily textured paving materials are used on the vehicular surface, smooth surface pedestrian paths and crossings must be provided.

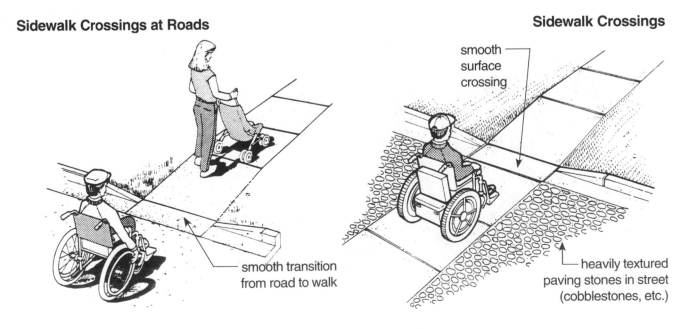

Sidewalk Crossings at Roads

smooth transition from road to walk

Sidewalk Crossings

smooth surface crossing

heavily textured paving stones in street (cobblestones, etc.)

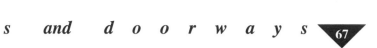Doors and doorways

continued on next page

Modifying Door Widths and Door Swing

Enlarging Door Widths

Door Widening

Changing Door Swing

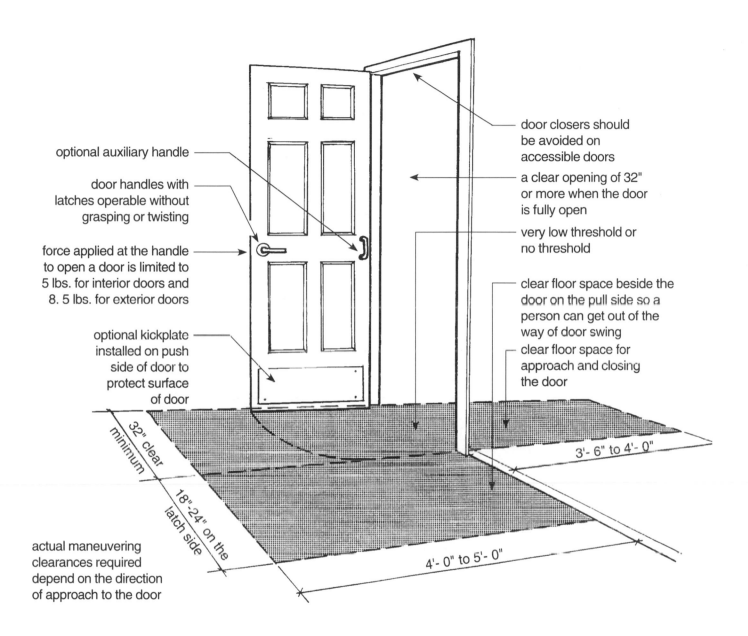

optional auxiliary handle

door handles with latches operable without grasping or twisting

force applied at the handle to open a door is limited to 5 lbs. for interior doors and 8. 5 lbs. for exterior doors

optional kickplate installed on push side of door to protect surface of door

door closers should be avoided on accessible doors

a clear opening of 32" or more when the door is fully open

very low threshold or no threshold

clear floor space beside the door on the pull side so a person can get out of the way of door swing

clear floor space for approach and closing the door

32" clear minimum

18"-24" on the latch side

3'- 6" to 4'- 0"

4'- 0" to 5'- 0"

actual maneuvering clearances required depend on the direction of approach to the door

Features of Accessible Doors and Doorways

Accessible doors must have certain features to be usable: 1) the doorway must be wide enough to pass through, 2) there must be adequate floor space in front of the door on both sides to open the door and close it, and to the side of the door where the handle and/or latch is located, 3) the threshold should be flush with the floor surface to prevent tripping and facilitate wheelchair passage, 4) the handle and/or latch must be operable without grasping, and 5) the door must be opened or closed with a minimal amount of effort.

Doorway Width

Door openings need to be wide enough to permit a person using a wheelchair, walker, or crutches to pass through without striking the door, door frame, or door hardware. Ideally, a door opening should be a few inches wider than wheelchairs. This allows space for hands and elbows, and provides maneuvering clearance necessary to pass through without bumping into the jambs. The clearance also provides space to pass through the door at an angle as it is sometimes impossible to align exactly and move straight through a doorway.

The two national design standards for accessibility, the American National Standards Institute's A117.1 (1986) (ANSI) and the Uniform Federal Accessibility Standard (UFAS) and most building codes specify a minimum 32 inch wide clear doorway opening. This means that there is at least a 32 inch space between the face of the door and the doorstop when the door is standing open 90 degrees.

A 2'-10" or a 3'-0" door is required to provide a 32 inch clear opening. The clear opening is always less than the full width of the door because the opening is reduced by 1) the thickness of the door, 2) the space between the door and the frame on the hinge side, and 3) by the thickness of the door stop molding on the door frame. Thus a 2'-8" door, having a clear opening of approximately 30 inches, does not provide the necessary clearance.

Clear Door Width

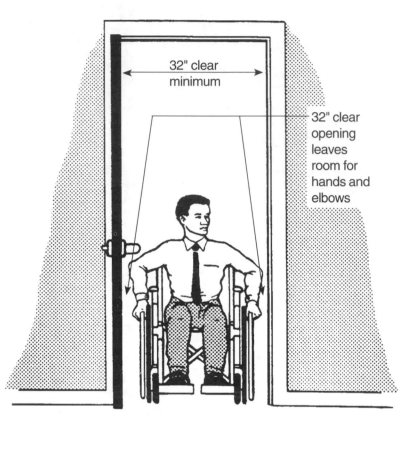

32" clear minimum

32" clear opening leaves room for hands and elbows

Measuring Clear Width

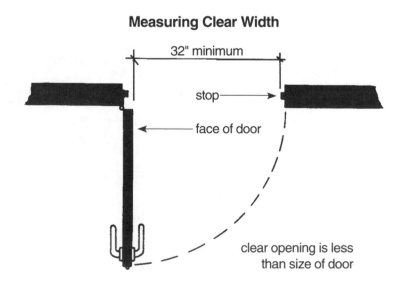

32" minimum

stop

face of door

clear opening is less than size of door

Clear Floor Space at Doors

narrower clear floor space on push side of the door

space to the side of the door to operate door latch, pull open the door, and get out of the way of the swing

larger clear floor space on the pull side of the door to provide space to open the door

Clear Floor Space

Clear unobstructed floor space is needed at doors to allow disabled people to maneuver into place to open or close a door. The space begins on the hinge side of the door, extends the width of the door and continues beyond the latch/handle side of the door. It also extends in front of the door to provide enough space to operate the handle/latch, open the door, and move out of the way of the door swing.

The size of the clear floor space needed depends on the door width, the direction of door swing, and the direction of movement on both sides of the door. For more specific information see ANSI or UFAS.

Clear Floor Space

Clear floor space on the pull side of doors must be larger than on the push side. The extra space on the pull side is necessary to permit a person to position themselves next to the door, beside the handle/lever, and out of the way of the swing of the door in order to pull it open. It is almost impossible for most mobility impaired people to hold onto a door handle/lever and back up at the same time. If the clear space is not provided, the door will hit the wheelchair or walker as it is opened preventing passage.

However, when clear space is provided to the front and side of a door, a wheelchair user can approach from the angle that best facilitates reaching and operating the door handle/latch, opening the door, then rotating slightly and proceeding through the doorway.

At least 18 inches, preferably 24 inches and, depending on the approach to the door, as much as 42 inches of clear space should be provided next to the handle/latch jamb on the pull side of the door. This clear area should also extend 4'-0" to 5'-0" from the wall depending on the type of approach to the door. On the push side of the door, clear area to the side can sometimes be eliminated and clear area in front of the door can be reduced to 3'-6" to 4'-0" depending on the

Clear Floor Space for a Front Approach

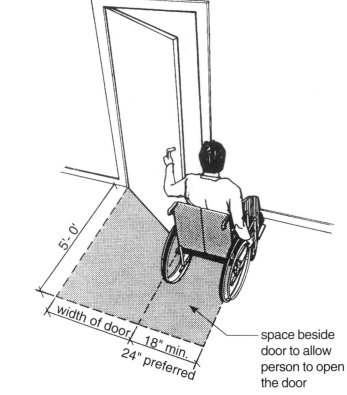

space beside door to allow person to open the door

approach. For clarification, see "Doors" section in ANSI or UFAS.

The necessary clear floor space on either side of a door must not be blocked by furniture or other items. The placement of a table, chest or chair near a doorway can significantly restrict the usability of a doorway.

Doors Without Adequate Space to the Side

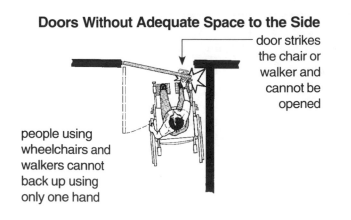

door strikes the chair or walker and cannot be opened

people using wheelchairs and walkers cannot back up using only one hand

Doors With Adequate Space to the Side

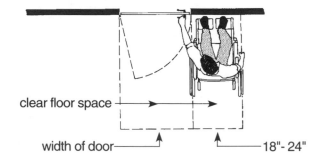

clear floor space

width of door⎯⎯⎯⎯⎯⎯⎯ 18"- 24"

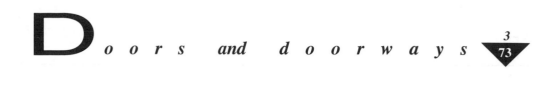

Use of Clear Floor Space

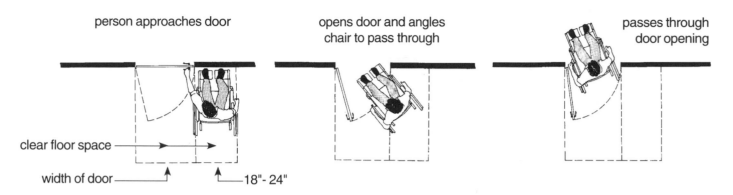

person approaches door

opens door and angles
chair to pass through

passes through
door opening

clear floor space

width of door —— 18"- 24"

Clear Floor Space
Hallways

The width of adjacent hallways and the width of the doorway are related and the combination of these elements determine whether wheelchair passage is possible. Enough clear space must exist at both the doorway and the hallway to permit a 90 degree turn. If a 32" clear door opening is provided, most people will be able to perform a 90 degree turn from a 3'-6" wide hallway into a room provided the door is inswinging. Turning into a hallway less than 3'-6" will be more difficult and will likely result in damage to the wall and door jambs.

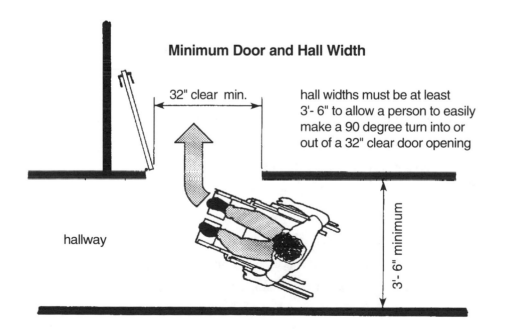

Minimum Door and Hall Width

32" clear min.

hall widths must be at least 3'- 6" to allow a person to easily make a 90 degree turn into or out of a 32" clear door opening

hallway

3'- 6" minimum

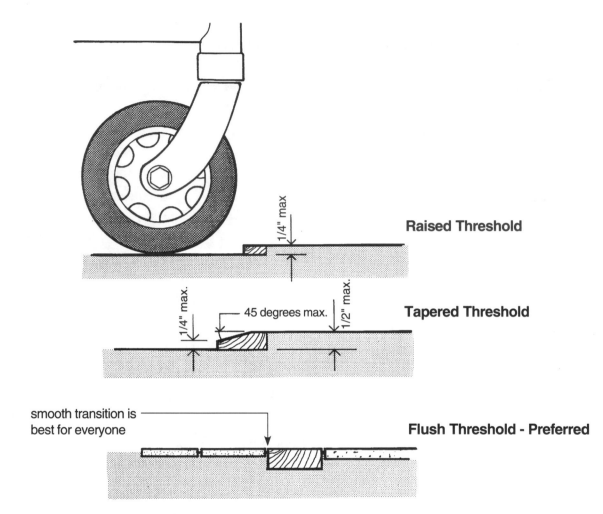

Raised Threshold

1/4" max

1/4" max. — 45 degrees max. — 1/2" max. **Tapered Threshold**

smooth transition is best for everyone **Flush Threshold - Preferred**

Thresholds

Raised thresholds are tripping hazards for many people and significant obstacles for people using wheelchairs. Whenever possible, thresholds should not be used or they should be installed flush with the flooring surface. If a threshold must be used, it should never have a level change more than 1/4" without being tapered. When a tapered threshold is used, the level change may be a maximum of 1/2". If a threshold represents a level change greater than 1/2", it is considered a ramp and must slope at 1" in 12" maximum.

Lever Handles on Doors with Latches

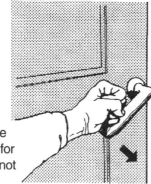

lever handles are
easy to operate for
people who cannot
grasp or twist

Push Plates on Doors with Latches

push plates require
no twisting or
grasping to operate

Loop Handles on Doors

Fixed Handles
Without Latches

Moveable Handles
With Latches

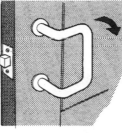

fixed loop
handles have
space to slide
hand behind

moveable
loops are easy
to operate

Door Hardware

People with limited use of their hands may have difficulty using traditional door handles, such as round knobs which require grasping and turning, or handles which require depressing a thumb lever to release the latch. The national standards specify that door handles must not require gripping or twisting or more than five pounds of force to release the latch. To comply with these standards, doors with handles should be operable with one hand without requiring grasping or twisting. A good test of the usability of a handle is to determine whether it is operable using a clenched fist or a completely opened hand.

Push plates and push bars are also generally quite usable on the push side of doors for operating latches. Movable loop handles or pull bars, used in commercial/multi-family residential applications on exterior doors, work well on the pull side, provided they have enough space for users to put their whole hand or wrist behind them. Round, square, or solid knobs or pulls and thumb levers should be avoided.

Doors without latches are most usable when equipped with pull bars or fixed loops. Similar to handles for doors with latches, handles for doors without latches should not require grasping and should be usable by persons with limited hand function.

Door Hardware

Modified Door Knobs

Door knobs can be adapted or changed to make them easier to use. Round knobs can be adapted by adding a plastic or metal lever handle over the existing knob. The lever clamps onto the knob and can be removed at a later date if not needed. They are available in different materials and colors.

Door Hardware

Replacement Lever Handles

A more permanent way to improve the usability of a door knob is to replace it with a lever handle. Most lever type handles meet the criteria for usable door handles.

There are two ways to install lever handles. The least expensive method involves removing the existing knobs and replacing them with matching lever handles. Some manufacturers are now making lever handle conversion kits to replace knobs. If replacement lever handles cannot be found that will fit and match the existing hardware, then the entire lockset will need to be replaced. A lockset consists of two handles, the interior mechanism, latch, strike plate and sometimes a lock.

Lever handle locksets are now available in a variety of styles, prices, and materials for residential use. They are attractive and usable by everyone.

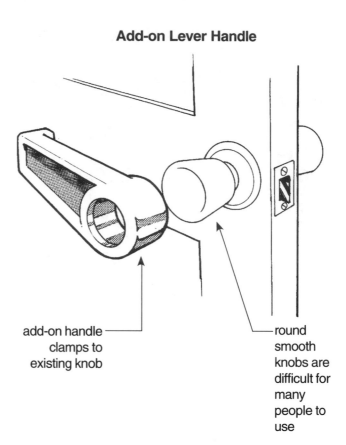

Add-on Lever Handle

add-on handle clamps to existing knob

round smooth knobs are difficult for many people to use

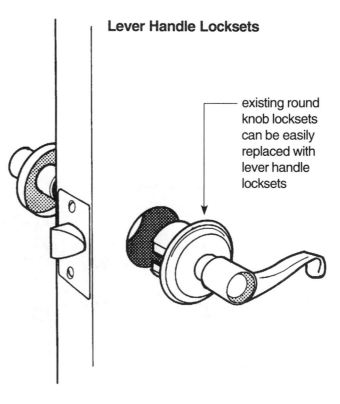

Lever Handle Locksets

existing round knob locksets can be easily replaced with lever handle locksets

Auxiliary Handle on Pull Side of Door

6" max.

auxiliary handle makes it easier to close the door

Door Hardware
Auxiliary Handles

Many mobility impaired people have difficulty closing doors from the push side because the knob or lever handle cannot be reached. A second handle or pulling device can be added to eliminate this problem. A 4 inch loop handle, like those used on drawers and kitchen cabinets, can be installed on the pull side of a door, near the hinge edge, to provide a place to pull the door closed.

Door Hardware
Locks and Keys

Many people with severe hand limitations cannot hold and use a standard key because it is too small for them to grasp. For some people a key "handle" can be made or purchased which makes it possible to grasp and control the key using the whole hand.

Push button combination locks are also a good choice for some people who have limited hand use.

Add-on Key "Handle"

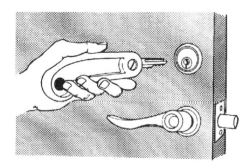

the addition of a key "handle" allows someone to grasp and control the key with their whole hand

Push Button Combination

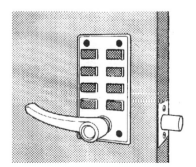

this type of lock works well for people who have little or no ability to twist or grasp

Little Force to Open Door

no more force than 5 lbs. at interior doors and 8.5 lbs. at exterior doors should be required to open a door

Force to Open Doors

In addition to the five pounds of force for operating controls, the national standards, ANSI and UFAS, also specify a maximum acceptable force for opening a door. This force, applied at the handle after the latch is released, should not exceed 8.5 pounds of force on exterior doors and 5 pounds of force on interior doors. This criteria applies to all types of interior and exterior doors including hinged doors, sliding doors, pocket doors, folding doors, etc.

A greater force is allowed on exterior doors to overcome the resistance created by weatherstripping, the additional weight of the door, and the pressure of springs or closers needed to keep them closed against the wind. For many people, however, a force of 8.5 pounds is too much and a lower force requirement should be used whenever possible. In extreme conditions, power operators may be installed to facilitate use.

Force to Open Doors
Power Door Opener

People with severe hand and arm limitations or diminished strength and agility may not be able to use any type of manually operated doors. Small motor driven power operators can be installed on exterior and interior single leaf hinged doors to help such users open doors independently. These power operators are also useful for anyone carrying packages or pushing strollers or carts.

Most power operators are fairly expensive because they are models designed for commercial use. However, some lower cost light duty models are made for home use. Low-energy, light duty, slow moving power door operators allow the door to be operated manually in the standard manner or power activated by those who need the assistance. They can be activated by wall, floor, or remote control switches. For safety, such door openers move slowly and stop if obstructed.

Most power operators attach to the door frame above the door and operate on standard house current. Doors requiring latches and or locks can be equipped with electric strike plates that unlock and release the latch the instant the operator switch is depressed. A variety of electronic lock devices can be installed on the operator switch for security.

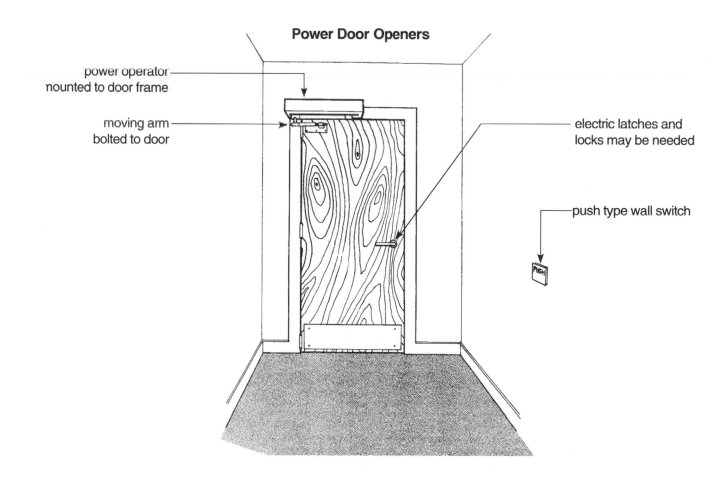

Power Door Openers

power operator mounted to door frame

moving arm bolted to door

electric latches and locks may be needed

push type wall switch

PUSH

Types of Doors

There are several distinct door types, some with overlapping features, which are commonly used in residential settings. These include hinged, sliding, pocket, bi-fold, folding, double, screen and storm doors. Some door types are generally easier for people to use than others. However, certain features of any door type can either facilitate or complicate the use of that particular door type by mobility impaired people.

Commonly Installed Hinged Door

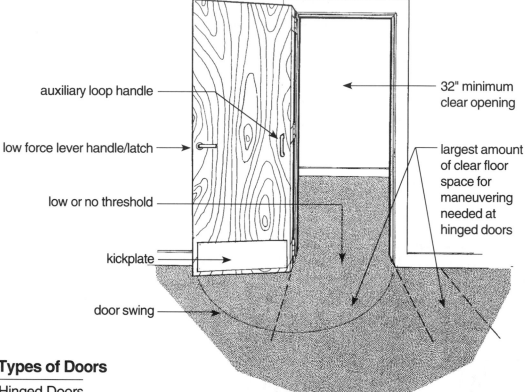

auxiliary loop handle

low force lever handle/latch →

low or no threshold

kickplate →

door swing

32" minimum clear opening

largest amount of clear floor space for maneuvering needed at hinged doors

Types of Doors

Hinged Doors

Hinged doors, which are the most common, are usable by most people. When properly configured and installed, a hinged door can be easy to open and close. Generally, the hinged doors which are easiest to use are those with no weatherstripping, door closers, or thresholds and those that have easy to use door hardware.

One problem with hinged doors is that the process of opening and closing the door requires a large amount of clear floor space. Access to the space behind the door is also limited when a hinged door is in the open position. These problems can sometimes be resolved by changing the swing of the door, creating additional floor space for maneuvering or by using another type of door.

Sliding Door

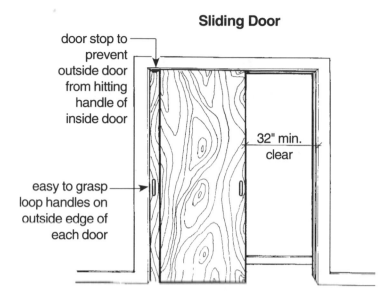

door stop to prevent outside door from hitting handle of inside door

easy to grasp loop handles on outside edge of each door

32" min. clear

Sliding or Pocket Door

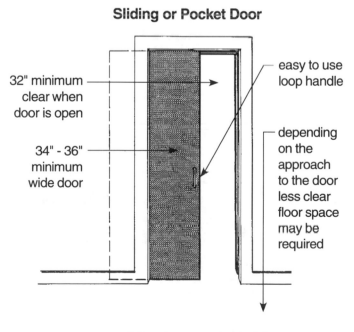

32" minimum clear when door is open

34" - 36" minimum wide door

easy to use loop handle

depending on the approach to the door less clear floor space may be required

sliding doors must stop fully open with their handles exposed and usable from both sides

Types of Doors
Sliding Doors

Sliding doors are sometimes used as closet doors. These doors are usually configured as overlapping panels which slide on a set of tracks. If used, sliding door assemblies should be of high quality to minimize maintenance problems. Although not required by UFAS or ANSI for non-passage doors, if the clear opening is at least 32" it facilitates easy access to the closet contents. If sliding doors are used, large loop handles should be installed.

Types of Doors
Pocket Doors

Many people recommend using "pocket" or hidden sliding doors to avoid the problems caused by the door swing. Pocket doors slide into a wall and are hidden when fully opened. Because the door does not swing out into the room, less clear floor space may be needed. However, pocket doors have some disadvantages. The door assembly is more expensive to purchase and install than hinged doors. Pocket doors also require periodic maintenance. The traditional handle and latch installed on pocket doors may be difficult to operate because they are recessed into the face of the door to allow the door to slide completely into the wall pocket. To facilitate use for people with limited hand function, loop handles, easy to use latches, and a doorstop can be installed which will prevent the door from sliding completely into the wall pocket. This configuration will require a wider door opening as the leading edge of the door will remain exposed in the open position.

Types of Doors

Bi-fold Door

Another type of door commonly found in homes is the bi-fold door, a set of hinged panels that fold together when opened. Bi-fold doors do not have as wide a door swing as a hinged door but they occupy more of the clear door opening. When the door is in the open position, the clear opening is reduced by 3" to 6", depending on the total number of panels in the door. Considering this, the smallest doorway in which a bi-fold assembly can be installed is 3'-0" wide.

Opening a bi-fold door requires less maneuvering space to the side of the door than is required to open a comparable hinged door. In addition, open bi-fold doors take up less floor space in the room than a hinged door. Bi-fold doors may not be as easy to open as hinged doors for some people because the door has to be pulled to the side as it is opened. A major problem with bi-fold doors is the tendency for the door to come off its track if bumped or pushed. It is therefore crucial that the door be carefully installed with appropriate hardware.

Bi-fold doors are commonly used at closets and should allow adequate access to the closet's contents. If installed, the door assembly should be of high quality and the clear opening should be at least 32" to facilitate easy access to the contents of the closet.

Bi-fold Door

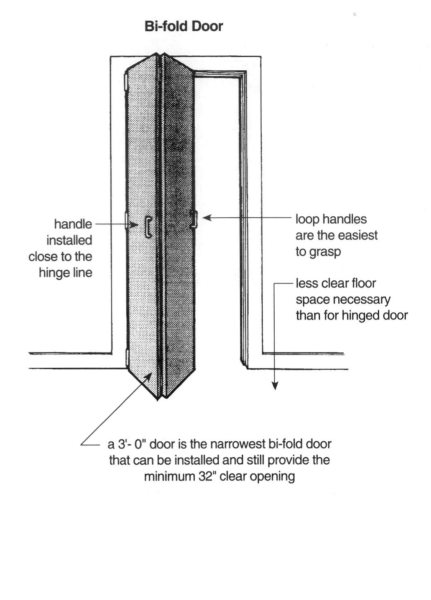

handle installed close to the hinge line

loop handles are the easiest to grasp

less clear floor space necessary than for hinged door

a 3'- 0" door is the narrowest bi-fold door that can be installed and still provide the minimum 32" clear opening

Plan of Bi-fold Door

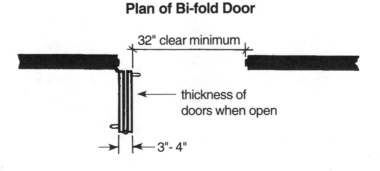

32" clear minimum

thickness of doors when open

3"- 4"

Folding Door

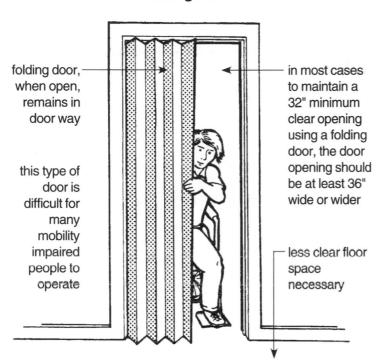

folding door, when open, remains in door way

this type of door is difficult for many mobility impaired people to operate

in most cases to maintain a 32" minimum clear opening using a folding door, the door opening should be at least 36" wide or wider

less clear floor space necessary

Double Leaf Door

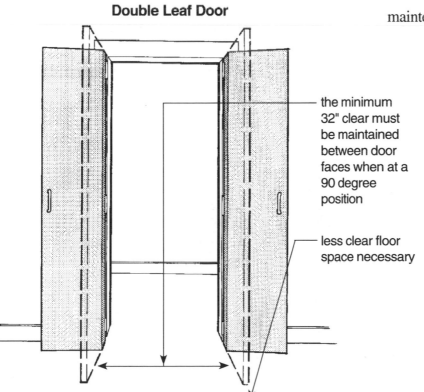

the minimum 32" clear must be maintained between door faces when at a 90 degree position

less clear floor space necessary

Types of Doors
Folding Doors

Folding doors are multiple panels attached or hinged together which function much like an accordion. Folding doors are sometimes difficult to operate because of their flexible construction. Since open folding doors occupy space in the doorway, the door opening will need to be wide enough to contain the folded door and still allow adequate passage space.

Folding doors come in a variety of materials and price ranges. Cheaper, lower quality folding doors will not function smoothly and will likely require frequent maintenance or replacement.

Types of Doors
Double Leaf

Two narrow double leaf doors mounted in a single frame may be slightly more difficult to open and close than a single wider door. Double leaf doors can be a useful choice where space for the door swing is limited and where doors are likely to stand open. If double doors are used, it is preferred that they be installed in a three foot minimum doorway.

Types of Doors

Screen and Storm Doors

Screen and storm doors are particularly difficult for many mobility impaired people because they must operate both doors at the same time. These doors can be eliminated where independent accessibility is more important. Screened porches and airlock double door vestibules which separate the protective door from the entrance door by at least 4'-0" can eliminate the problem.

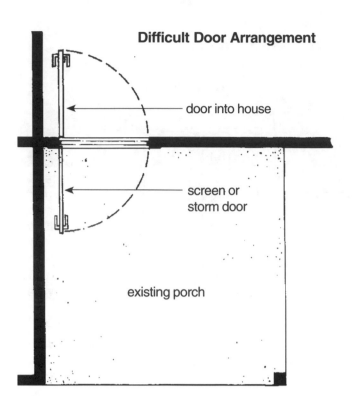

Difficult Door Arrangement

door into house

screen or storm door

existing porch

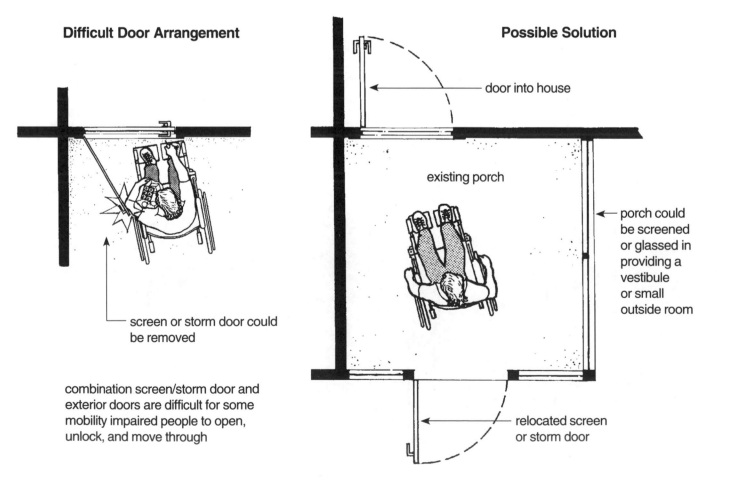

Difficult Door Arrangement

screen or storm door could be removed

combination screen/storm door and exterior doors are difficult for some mobility impaired people to open, unlock, and move through

Possible Solution

door into house

existing porch

porch could be screened or glassed in providing a vestibule or small outside room

relocated screen or storm door

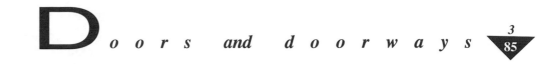
Remove the Door to Temporarily Increase the Clear Opening

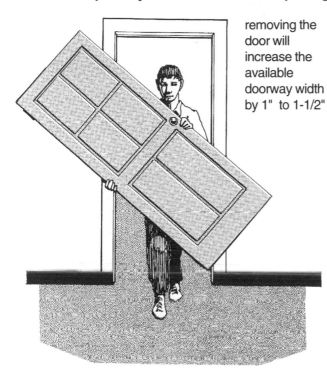

removing the door will increase the available doorway width by 1" to 1-1/2"

Install Swing-away Hinges to Permanently Increase the Clear Opening

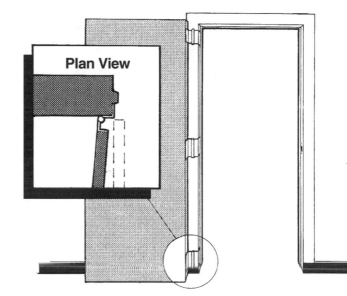

Plan View

swing-away hinges allow the door to swing out of the door opening and increase the clear space by 1" to 1-1/2"

Swing Away Hinges

Modifying Door Widths and Door Swing
Enlarging Door Widths

There are at least three ways that clear width in existing doorways can be widened: 1) the door can be removed, 2) special hinges can be installed to provide more clearance, or 3) the door can be permanently replaced with a larger door.

To temporarily increase the width by 1 or 1- 1/2 inches the door can be removed. Some people do this and install a curtain to provide limited privacy. Removing the door will help only when the door opening is almost wide enough for a wheelchair to pass through.

When removal of the door is undesirable, a more permanent solution is to install swing-away hinges. Like standard hinges, these hinges permit the door to swing open but provide additional clearance. The door can be opened 90 degrees or more allowing the door to be completely out of the doorway. Installing swing-away hinges can increase the clear space by as much as 1 - 1/2".

Door Widening - Wood Frame Wall

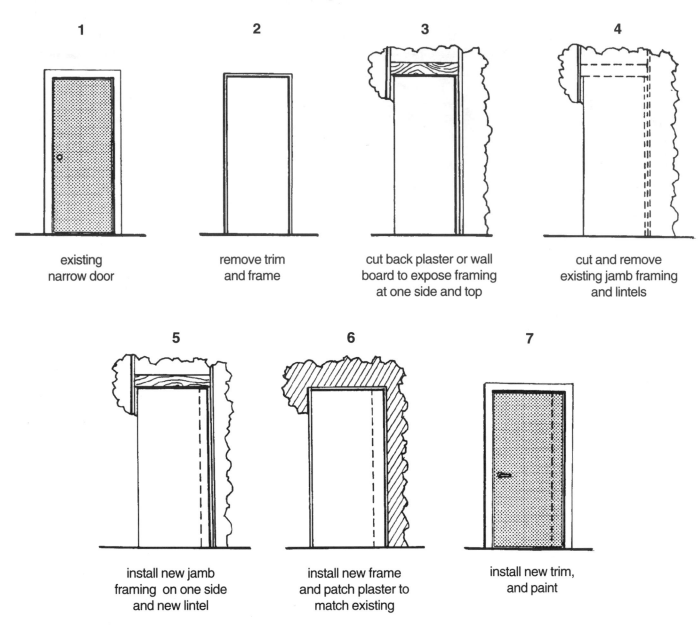

1 existing narrow door

2 remove trim and frame

3 cut back plaster or wall board to expose framing at one side and top

4 cut and remove existing jamb framing and lintels

5 install new jamb framing on one side and new lintel

6 install new frame and patch plaster to match existing

7 install new trim, and paint

Modifying Door Widths and Door Swing

Door Widening

If removing the door or using a swing-away hinge is not feasible, then enlarging the doorway and replacing the door may be considered. This sometimes involves altering the structure of the home so it is best to consult a qualified contractor, engineer, or architect before starting.

Door widening in typical wood frame walls will require removing existing jambs and some framing studs, cutting back the plaster or sheetrock, bracing overhead supports and replacing the entire assembly with new material. The plaster will have to be repaired and the wall repainted. The exposed floor will need finishing as well. This can be a messy process and should be considered carefully before undertaking.

Reversing Swing of Door Improves Access to Bathtub

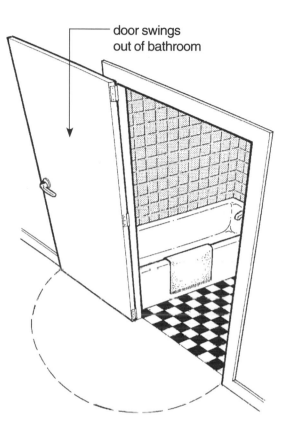

door swings
out of bathroom

when reversing the swing of a
door, the hinges may need to
be flipped, the latch moved,
and the doorstop relocated

Modifying Door Widths and Door Swing

Changing Door Swing

Hinged doors consume valuable floor space on the pull side and obstruct access to the space behind the door in the open position. This problem is most noticeable in small rooms like bathrooms. Frequently this problem can be corrected by reversing the swing of the door so that it swings out of the room. This works especially well when the door opens out into a hallway or against clear wall where the door can be opened all the way.

Reversing the swing of a door may require flipping the hinges to the opposite side of the jamb and door, reversing the position of the strike plate on the jamb, removing and turning over the latch bolt in the door, replacing or relocating the doorstop, and finally filling and painting the original hinge mounting holes.

Inswinging Door Blocks Access to Bathtub

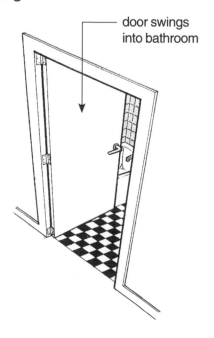

door swings
into bathroom

W *i n d o w s*

windows that are easy to
open and close with one hand

window
lock and
operator
within
reach of
seated
person

clear floor space
approach to windows

Features of Accessible Windows

To be usable by mobility impaired people (people who use crutches,
canes, walkers, or wheelchairs), windows must have several features: 1)
a clear floor space available at each window so a person can maneuver and
get close enough to operate the window, 2) window lock(s) and operator
within comfortable reach, and 3) lock(s), operator, and window sash (one
half of a double hung window), which is easy to open with one hand.

Clear Floor Space

Many mobility impaired people need clear floor space in front of operable windows. The clear floor space allows the person to maneuver to get close enough to open, close, or lock the window. The minimum size of clear floor space at windows for wheelchair users is 2'- 6" x 4'- 0". This clear floor space provided for wheelchair users is adequate for ambulatory people using crutches, walkers, or canes. The clear floor space may be located perpendicular to the window or parallel to the window.

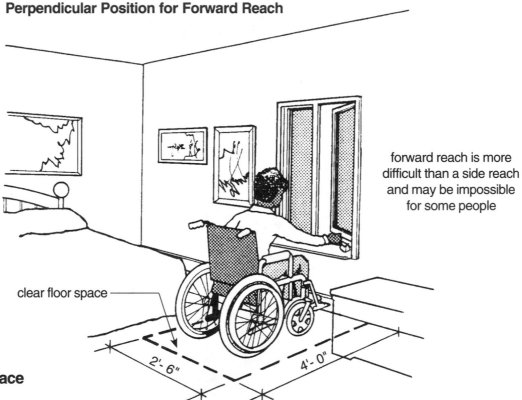

Perpendicular Position for Forward Reach

forward reach is more difficult than a side reach and may be impossible for some people

clear floor space

2'- 6"

4'- 0"

Clear Floor Space

Forward Reach

When the clear floor area is perpendicular to the window, a person in a wheelchair can only make a forward approach to the window which requires the user to stretch and lean forward to operate the window. This requirement limits what the person will be able to reach and consequently how well they will be able to open or close the window. Perpendicular clear floor spaces may be considered if space is limited and/or if awning or casement windows are used. It should be avoided, if possible, with double hung or sliding windows.

Parallel Position for Side Reach

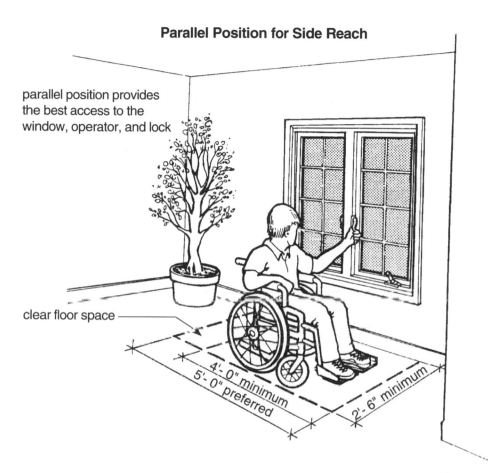

parallel position provides the best access to the window, operator, and lock

clear floor space

4'- 0" minimum
5'- 0" preferred

2'- 6" minimum

Clear Floor Space

Side Reach

Conversely, the parallel position, which is generally preferred, allows users to reach to the side to operate windows. Side reach is best for most people because they can get closer to the window, reach higher, and usually exert more force. The side approach is almost essential for operating double hung windows and is also best for operating blinds and draperies. When possible, clear floor space for a side reach should be provided at all windows.

To complete a side approach, a wheelchair user pulls up to the window diagonally and then moves forward and backward until positioned parallel to the window. Once in that position, the wheelchair user can usually reach to the side to open or close the window. To allow extra space for maneuvering, it is best if the clear floor space for side reach is increased from the minimum 2'- 6" x 4'-0" to 2'-6" x 5'-0".

Window Height

Depending on the room and the location of the window, the sill should be positioned between 18 inches and 36 inches above the floor so that a seated person can easily open or close the window. If possible, the window's vertical dimension should be such that it permits a view of the outdoors for both seated and standing people.

Generally, the height at which a window is positioned in the wall will dictate the location of the lock and operator and affect the window's ease of operation. For many people who use wheelchairs, the upper limit of their reach range is approximately 4'-0" for a forward reach and 4'-6" for a side reach. Because of these reach limits many wheelchair users prefer a lower operating handle and lock location. Handles and locks are easiest to use if they are positioned between 1'-6" and 3'-6" above the floor.

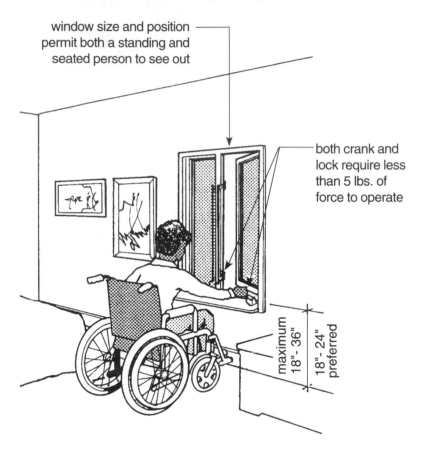

Low Window Sill and Operating Mechanism

window size and position permit both a standing and seated person to see out

both crank and lock require less than 5 lbs. of force to operate

maximum 18" - 36"

18" - 24" preferred

Force to Operate Windows and Locks

To comply with the ANSI standard, windows that must be opened or closed by pushing, pulling, or lifting must not require more that 5 pounds of force to operate. This maximum acceptable force for opening a window applies to all windows including double hung, sliding, casement, and awning. In addition, any operators or cranks used to open and close the window and any window locks must not require grasping, twisting, or fine hand movements, nor more than 5 pounds of force to operate. Cranks and locks should function easily and require use of only one hand for smooth operation.

A window unit should be carefully selected to match a user's preference and ability. Particular attention should be paid to the operator or crank and the lock. Window locks that are small and/or recessed into the window frame should be carefully evaluated and perhaps avoided.

Types of Windows

There are several distinct operable window types used in residential construction. Like other building products, the quality of windows varies widely. Less expensive, lower quality windows are generally less energy efficient and require more frequent repair and possible replacement. All windows do require regular maintenance in order to function properly.

Some types of windows are more easily used by mobility impaired people.

Double Hung Windows Are Difficult for Many Seated and Standing People to Open and Close

Types of Windows

Single and Double Hung Windows

The most common windows found in homes are single and double hung windows. These windows have two glass panels or sashes. To open the window, the bottom sash is lifted and slid along a track. In double hung windows, the upper sash is also moveable and can be lowered. Many people have trouble opening and closing single and double hung windows. These windows usually require high strength and gripping ability because of their weight and their tendency to stick and jam in the track. However, high quality single and double hung windows with well designed handles may be useable by some mobility impaired people.

The operation of double hung windows can sometimes be improved by adding a handle to the middle of the bottom sash where it meets the window sill. This handle may make it possible to lift the window using one hand. It also provides a gripping surface for closing the window and may allow even pressure to be applied on the sash preventing it from becoming crooked and getting stuck.

Auxiliary Handle

addition of an auxiliary handle makes it possible to open and close some windows with only one hand

Sliding Windows Are Easier for Some People to Use

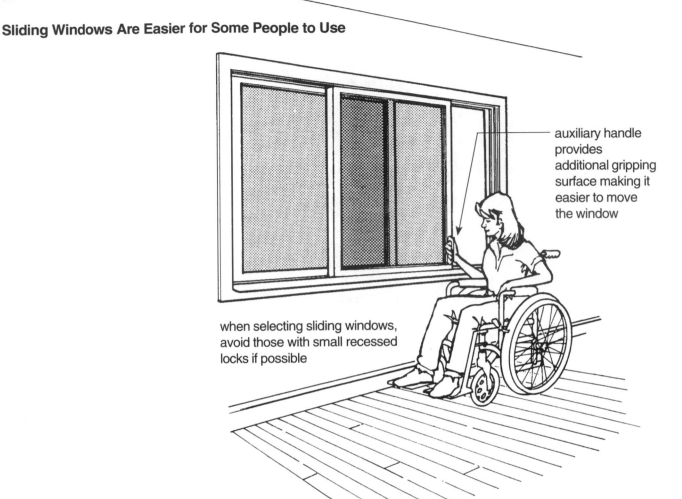

auxiliary handle provides additional gripping surface making it easier to move the window

when selecting sliding windows, avoid those with small recessed locks if possible

Types of Windows

Sliding Windows

Many people find that sliding windows are easier to use than double hung windows. Generally, sliding windows move more readily than double hung windows because they roll on a track. Unlike double hung windows, this design does not require the user to lift the weight of the window. Rather, the user pushes or pulls the glass panel along the track. Because the window panel rolls in the track, some maintenance is required to keep the track clean and free of debris.

An added benefit of sliding windows is that the lock is usually mounted at the bottom of the frame within reach. An auxiliary loop handle can be added to the frame of the sliding panel to facilitate use by people with limited hand function.

Casement Windows Are Among the Easiest to Operate

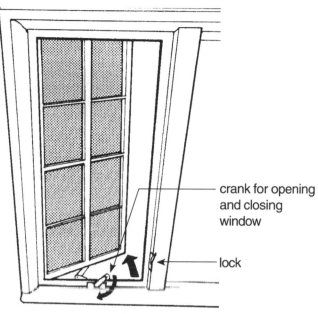

crank for opening
and closing
window

lock

Types of Windows
Casement Windows

Casement or awning windows are two of the easiest window types to operate. The main advantage of these windows is that the window is operated by a crank handle which many people can turn. Casement windows typically use a lever lock mounted along the vertical frame. One drawback of larger casement windows is that some have dual locks which may be difficult for seated people to open because the upper lock is out of reach. Some manufacturers do make an add-on linkage which can be attached to connect both the upper and lower locks to make them operable from the lower lock (see illustration).

Large Casement Windows with Dual Locks Are Easy to Operate if Add-on Linkage Is Provided

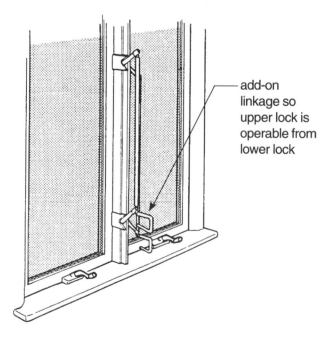

add-on
linkage so
upper lock is
operable from
lower lock

Types of Windows

Awning Windows

Awning windows have an advantage over casement windows because the window lock is part of the operating mechanism. When the window crank is turned to open the window, the lock is disengaged as the window opens. The lock is automatically engaged as the window is closed.

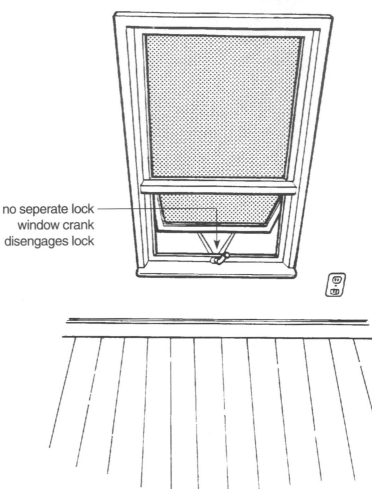

Awning Windows Are Easy to Operate

no seperate lock
window crank
disengages lock

Types of Windows

Storm Windows

Storm windows can only be used on sliding and double hung windows. Generally, they significantly complicate window operation and may not be operable by many mobility impaired people. Of the possible options, sliding windows with sliding storm windows (if they could be fabricated) seem likely to be the most useable.

Power Operators Are Available for Some
Casement, Awning, and Sliding Windows

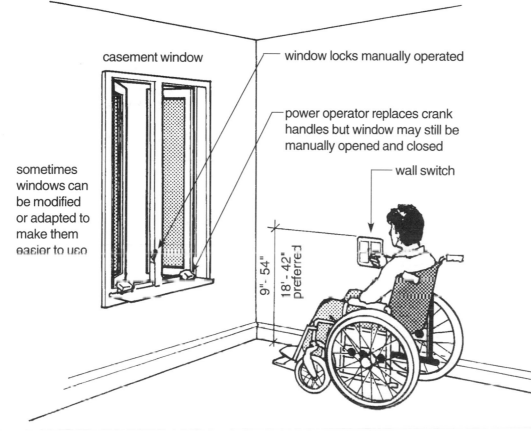

casement window

window locks manually operated

power operator replaces crank handles but window may still be manually opened and closed

wall switch

sometimes windows can be modified or adapted to make them easier to use

9" - 54"

18' - 42" preferred

Improving Use of Windows
Power Operators

For some people, it is difficult or impossible to open or close a window using theirs hands. Power operators which provide remote opening and closing capability are now available for some casement and awning windows. A small power operator for aluminum sliding windows is also available.

The power operator is mounted in place of the crank handle on the casement or awning window. When activated by a special wall switch, the motor opens the window to the desired position. Some units also have a water sensor that will automatically close the window if it rains.

If there is a power failure or if the motor fails, there is an auxiliary crank on the operator that permits the window to be closed manually. Power operators can be installed with a new window or as an adaptation to some existing windows.

Improving Use of Windows

Window Inserts

Where existing windows are inadequate, some people have built secondary window inserts inside the opening of a double hung window. The window insert could be made of two hinged panels as shown in the accompanying illustration or could be an awning or sliding insert. The window insert is supported from above by the existing window and if necessary, from the side by temporary framing. If an awning type insert is used, the original exterior screen must be removed to allow the awning to open. An interior screen can then be added as protection from insects. If a sliding insert is installed, the original exterior screen can remain in place. Inserts can be installed during the warm months and removed before colder weather.

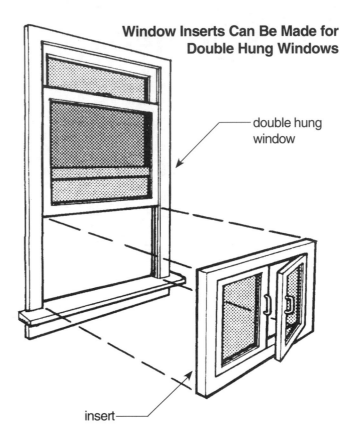

Window Inserts Can Be Made for Double Hung Windows

double hung window

insert

Improving Use of Windows

Replacement Windows

The most obvious, albeit costly, solution to problem windows is to replace them. If a window is too difficult to operate, and repair or replacement of parts will not result in a workable solution, then the window may need to be replaced with one that can be easily operated.

Windows as Emergency Exits

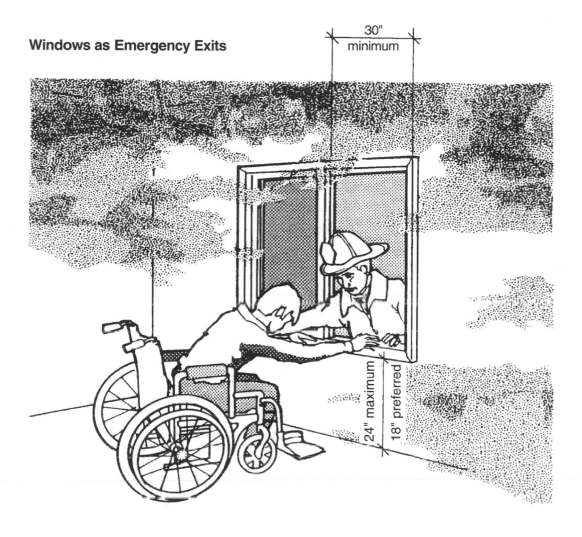

30"
minimum

24" maximum
18" preferred

Windows as Exits

In the event of fire or other emergency, it is sometimes necessary to use windows as exits. This is particularly true of bedrooms which may be remotely located from an exterior door. Windows providing an opening of at least 30" are generally wide enough to permit a person to pass through in an emergency. Since wheelchair seat height is generally at 18", window sills located no higher than 24" above the floor will allow someone using a wheelchair to transfer onto the window sill, or be easily lifted up onto the sill, and then helped out through the window. If screens are installed on emergency egress windows, they should be easily and quickly removeable.

K *itchens* 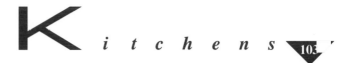 103

continued on next page

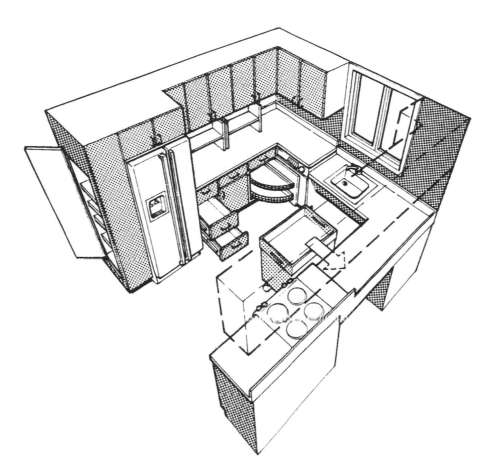

Features of Accessible Kitchens

Kitchens are one of the focal points of any house design. They require careful planning and design to be useable, safe, and comfortable. This is particularly true for people with disabilities.

Kitchen features are not the same for all disabled users. For some individuals with disabilities, unique details or arrangements may be needed to meet their particular requirements. In these cases, a custom design works best. For other people with disabilities, useful features can be generalized. The following kitchen design information is provided as general guidelines for three broad categories of people with disabilities: mobility impaired, visually impaired, and hearing impaired.

Designing a completely functional kitchen for people with mobility impairments requires more attention to details and space requirements. The category of mobility impaired includes; a) people who have walking or standing limitations which require them to sit down while performing some tasks, b) people who use crutches, canes or walkers to move about, and c) wheelchair users.

For both standing and sitting mobility impaired users, the key design issues include adequate maneuvering space and the installation of features within a designated reach range.

For both visually and hearing impaired users, the key design issues revolve around appropriate signals and controls.

Parallel Approach

Perpendicular or Forward Approach

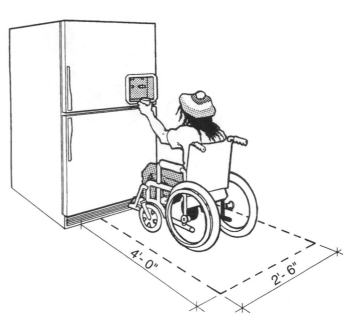

Maneuvering Space

In accessible kitchens, space must be provided for wheelchair users to maneuver close enough to cabinets and appliances to reach the knobs and controls which operate the devices. Each feature must have a minimum 2'- 6" x 4'- 0" clear floor area, arranged for either parallel or perpendicular approach in a wheelchair. Whenever possible, it is preferred that space for both parallel and perpendicular (forward) approaches be provided. Clear floor spaces may extend under countertops and into knee spaces a maximum of 19" (see section on "Knee Spaces").

Both Parallel and Forward Approaches Preferred

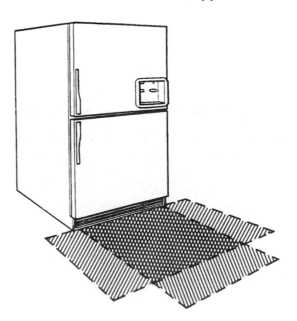

Knee Space

For people who must sit while performing kitchen tasks, knee spaces will be necessary to allow them to pull up under the work surface and sit close enough to reach items and work comfortably. Knee spaces may be needed under sinks, countertop segments, cook tops, and beside ranges, built-in ovens, and dishwashers.

In general, the minimum size of knee spaces is 30" wide, 27" high, and 19" deep. However in dwellings where adjustable features are installed, the height of the knee space varies. The preferred size is 3'- 0" wide because this larger dimension creates an additional turning space. This turning space is especially convenient for people using wheelchairs to maneuver about in small kitchens.

The knee space is best if unobstructed. However, disposals and plumbing traps may occupy some of the knee space under sinks. These devices should be insulated, padded, or concealed behind a panel, to prevent skin contact with hot or sharp surfaces.

Knee Spaces Are a Necessity for Seated Kitchen Users

Minimum Knee Space at Work Surfaces

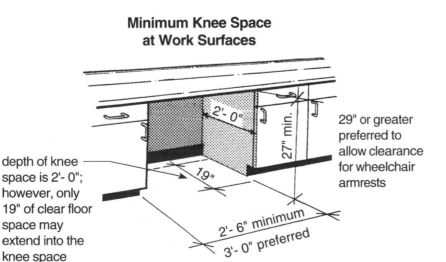

depth of knee space is 2'- 0"; however, only 19" of clear floor space may extend into the knee space

2'- 0"

27" min.

19"

2'- 6" minimum

3'- 0" preferred

29" or greater preferred to allow clearance for wheelchair armrests

Minimum Knee Space at Sinks

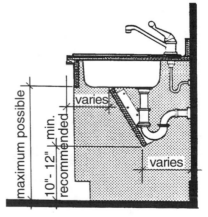

maximum possible

10"- 12" min. recommended

varies

varies

Turnaround Space

There should be sufficient space in or immediately adjacent to all kitchens to allow people using wheelchairs to turn around 180 degrees. Two types of clear floor spaces will make such turns possible: 1) a 5'-0" circular area, and 2) a 3' x 3' T-shaped area.

Each of these spaces allows a different type of turn to be made and each can drastically affect the design of any kitchen.

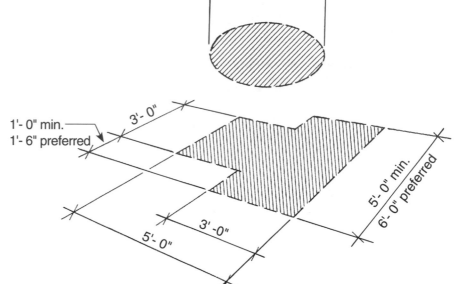

Clear Floor Spaces for Turning Wheelchairs

5'- 0" diameter

1'- 0" min.
1'- 6" preferred

3'- 0"

3'-0"

5'- 0"

5'- 0" min.
6'- 0" preferred

Turnaround Space

The Pivoting Turn

The 5'-0" diameter turning space provides a clear floor area to complete a 360 degree pivoting turn. For the average manual wheelchair user, the three dimensional space required for this turn resembles a wedding cake. The portion of the space closest to the floor must be 5'-0" in diameter. At approximately 1'-0" above the floor the diameter gets smaller and at 2'-6" it gets even smaller.

This can be useful information for planning economical yet accessible kitchens. The 1'-0" and 2'-6" high portions of the turning space can be provided under overhanging cabinets and tables or in knee spaces under countertops.

Clear Floor Space for a Pivoting or Circular Turn

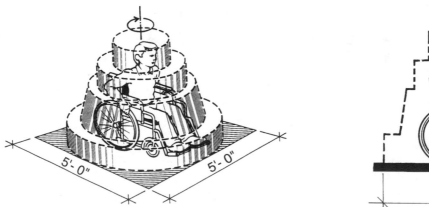

5'- 0"   5'- 0"

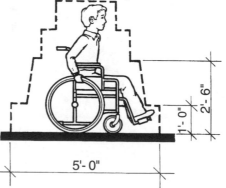

2'- 6"

1'- 0"

5'- 0"

Turnaround Space
The Pivoting Turn

Where ample space is available in the kitchen, the full 5'-0" diameter turning space is best for maneuvering between cabinets or between cabinets and walls.

Applying the previously described wedding cake analogy, a minimum 1'- 0" high x 6" deep toe space can be substituted for 6" of the turning space when space is limited. In very small kitchens, as much as 19"of the 5'-0" turning space can be part of the knee space under tables or countertops. To make it possible to perform a 360 degree turn in a wheelchair, the customary minumum-sized knee space width of 2'- 6" must be increased to a minimum of 4'-0" to 4'- 6".

5' Between Cabinet Fronts Preferred

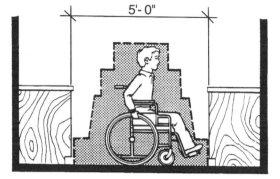

Clear Turning Space Between Cabinets with Enlarged Toe Space

Clear Turning Space Between Cabinets with Wider Than Minimum Knee Space

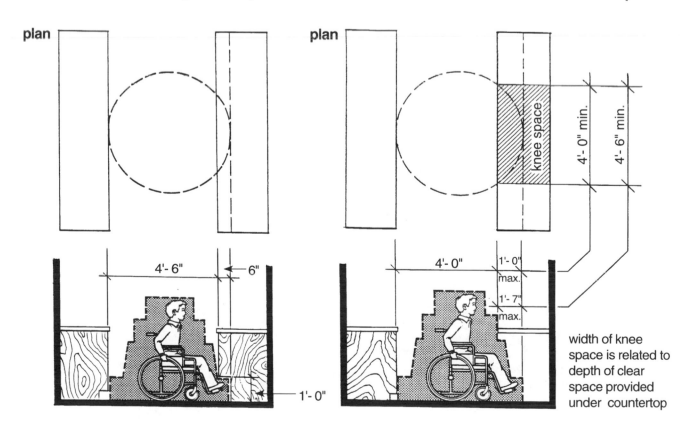

width of knee space is related to depth of clear space provided under countertop

Turnaround Space
The Pivoting Turn

In particularly small and simple kitchens, such as the "shotgun" or parallel plan, the 5'-0" diameter turning space could be located at either end of the cabinets. This placement might save space in the kitchen but will require the user to leave the kitchen area to turn around.

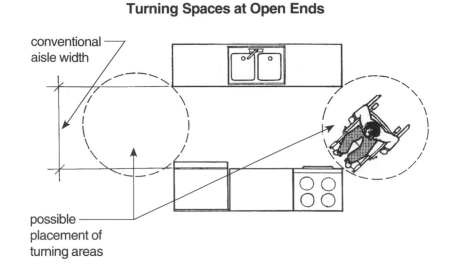

Very Small Kitchens with Turning Spaces at Open Ends

conventional aisle width

possible placement of turning areas

Turnaround Space
The T-Turn

The T-shaped turning space allows a three point turn to be made by pulling into one arm of the "T" and backing out into the other. This move is similar to turning an automobile around by pulling into a driveway and backing out.

By making one of the necessary kitchen knee spaces 3'- 0" wide, rather than the minimum 2'- 6", one leg of the "T" can be placed within the knee space. This arrangement saves considerable space and can eliminate any need to enlarge kitchens for accessibility.

T-Turn Within a Knee Space

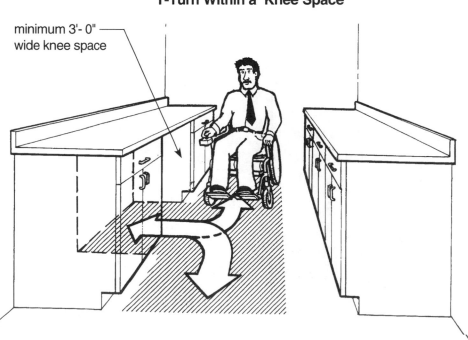

minimum 3'- 0" wide knee space

Kitchen Space Planning

Clear floor spaces at appliances, turning spaces, and knee spaces can be located as needed in any kitchen design to provide accessibility. They can overlap with each other to conserve space and, if carefully planned, they need not necessarily increase the size of a kitchen.

The maneuvering spaces discussed here are generally adequate for most people who use conventional manual or power wheelchairs. They are also adequate for people who use ordinary stationary chairs to sit while working in the kitchen and for people who use walkers or crutches and braces.

It must be noted that these are minimum spaces which may not be convenient when more than one person is using the kitchen at the same time. In families where active participation by members with disabilities occurs, kitchen planning should take this into account. Additional space, consistent with good design practice and affordability, should be included to accommodate all participants.

The maneuvering spaces shown here may not be adequate for mobility impaired people who use one of the three wheeled electrically powered scooters popular today. Generally, scooters are not as maneuverable as conventional wheelchairs and many models may require additional maneuvering space. An individual space analysis should be conducted when designing a kitchen for a person who uses such special equipment .

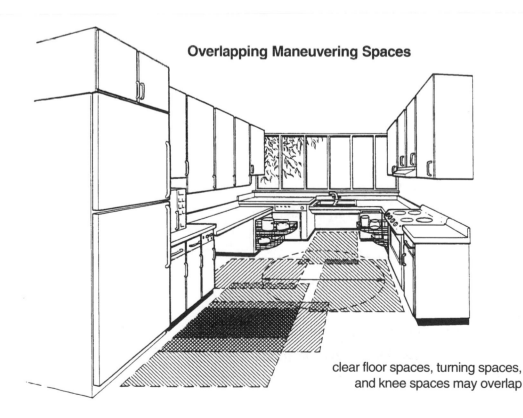

Overlapping Maneuvering Spaces

clear floor spaces, turning spaces,
and knee spaces may overlap

Heights and Reach Ranges

Mobility impaired people who use wheelchairs or who sit down while performing kitchen tasks, have a forward reach range of approximately 15" to 48" above the floor. This limited reach range makes most conventional base cabinets and wall cabinet storage unusable by seated people. Some seated people can reach to approximately 4'-6" above the floor if they can turn to one side and position themselves very close to the storage shelving.

Standing mobility impaired people have slightly different reach limitations. Many people are able to reach at least the lower level shelves of conventional wall cabinets but, because of limited ability to bend over or stoop down, they may be unable to use low and rear portions of base cabinet storage. Another factor which often complicates use for standing mobility impaired people is their need to use their arms and hands to maintain balance. As such, they may have difficulty reaching and lifting objects that are extremely low or high.

For standing mobility impaired people, a suggested reach range which addresses these factors is 2'-0" to 6'-0" above the floor.

There are storage and other design options which compensate for limited reach ranges and allow features to be used by both standing and seated mobility impaired people. These techniques are described elsewhere in this section.

Reach Range for Seated People at Knee Spaces

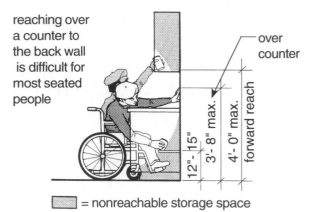

reaching over a counter to the back wall is difficult for most seated people

= nonreachable storage space

Maximum Side Reach Range for Seated People at Shelving

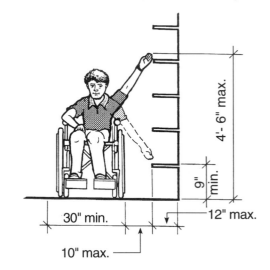

Suggested Maximum and Minimum Reach Heights for Standing Mobility Impaired People

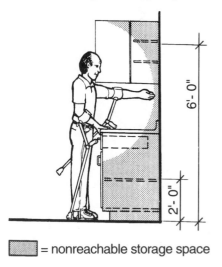

= nonreachable storage space

Counter Heights

Standard kitchen counters are 3'- 0" high. This height is usually too high for seated people but is generally adequate for both disabled and non-disabled standing people. Counter heights of 30", 32", and 34" are more comfortable for seated people to use for food preparation, cooking, and clean-up. The issue of "best height" complicates the design of kitchens when used by both standing and seated people.

Common solutions include: 1) counters at a maximum height of 34" or lower, which will place counters at a height that is uncomfortable and awkward for many standing people, 2) providing some segments at standard height and some at lower heights, or 3) installing motor driven adjustable height counters, including sinks and cooktops, that can be raised or lowered instantly at the touch of a button. This situation dictates some arrangement of dual heights to accommodate all users.

Typical Lowered Counter Segments

30"- 34" high lowered work surface or desk; 30" minimum width, 36" or wider preferred

standard 3'- 0" counter at dishwasher and other appliances

lowered sink counter segment

clear knee space

pipe protection and appearance panel

Counter Heights

Uniform Height

A uniform lowered height may not be an ideal solution because it is somewhat inconvenient for standing users. Appliances such as dishwashers, trash compactors and ranges are designed for 3'- 0" counter heights; therefore, some counter segments will have to remain at the standard height even if the remainder are set at a lowered height.

Counter Heights

Dual Height Counter

Dual height kitchens generally include lowered counter segments to provide work surfaces for seated people. Sinks and cooktops can also be placed in the lowered segments to make cooking and clean-up more comfortable for seated people. To be useful to seated people, each lowered counter segment must have a clear knee space below (see "Knee Spaces"). If sinks, other plumbing fixtures, or cooktops are installed in the lowered segments, protective/appearance panels or enclosures should be installed (see "Sinks").

An important consideration in setting the counter height for lowered segments is the clear height of the knee space below. 30" of clear vertical space at the front edge of the counter will usually provide enough clearance for the arm rests of most wheelchairs and is therefore preferred. The access standards, American National Standards Institute ANSI A117.1(1986) and the Uniform Federal Access Standards (UFAS), stipulate a 27" minimum.

Many wheelchairs have "desk arms" where the front of the arm rest drops down to approximately 25". Others have "sport model arms" that slope from rear to front. Both types will fit under lower counters and require less knee space clearance. When designing a kitchen for a particular wheelchair user, determination of the type of chair may allow more flexibility in setting heights and clearances.

Standard Arm Wheelchair

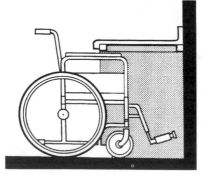

Desk Arm Wheelchair

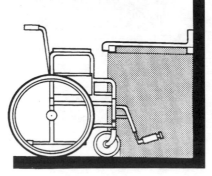

Sport Model Wheelchair

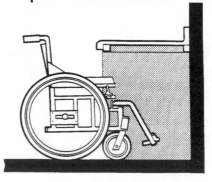

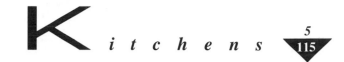

Counter Heights

Electrically Adjustable Height

Motor driven adjustable height kitchen counters are perhaps the ideal functional solution where the same kitchen will be used on a daily basis by both standing and seated members of the same household. By activating a switch, an electrically powered system can raise and lower counters, base cabinets, and wall cabinets. Use of flexible or slip joint plumbing and wiring in flexible conduit allows sinks and cooktop counter segments to be adjusted as well. Specific elements move as a unit and are instantly and infinitely adjustable to the individual user's ideal height. They can be lowered to facilitate reaching for items in overhead cabinets and raised again for food preparation or to the "best looking" height.

The additional cost of these manufactured systems may be justified where kitchen use and independence are high family priorities, where frequent changes in kitchen users are common, or where there is likely to be a high turnover of disabled occupants.

Motor Driven Adjustable Height Kitchen Cabinets

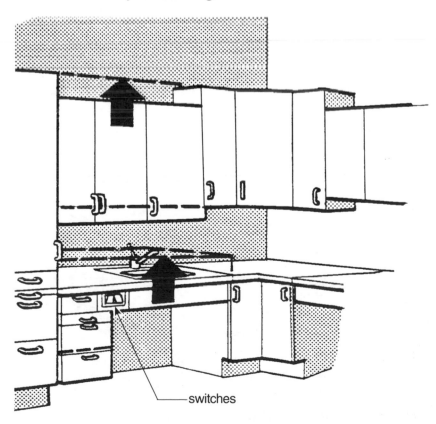

switches

Counter Heights

Manually Adjustable Counter Segments

Counter segments can also be made adjustable in height using shelf hardware or movable blocking. Once designed and finished for this purpose, these segments can be adjusted in height in a short time with no additional cost for renovations.

This approach is part of a concept called "adaptable design" which is most applicable in rental housing. Adaptable design requires that some features be adjustable to meet the changing needs of multiple tenants over the life of the dwelling. Features are intended for regular adjustment as tenants change but not for daily or frequent adjustment.

**Movable Wood Support
Strips for Adjusting Counter Height**

**Lowered Counter Attached
to Movable Wood Support Strips**

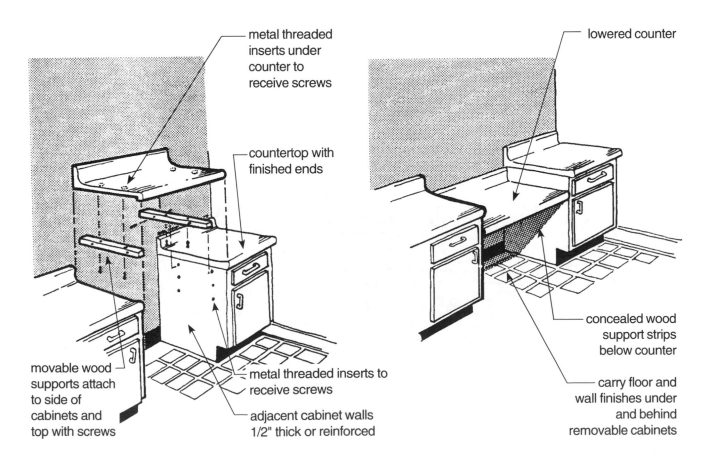

metal threaded
inserts under
counter to
receive screws

countertop with
finished ends

movable wood
supports attach
to side of
cabinets and
top with screws

metal threaded inserts to
receive screws

adjacent cabinet walls
1/2" thick or reinforced

lowered counter

concealed wood
support strips
below counter

carry floor and
wall finishes under
and behind
removable cabinets

Counter Heights

Manually Adjustable Counter Segments

Adaptable design was conceived as a marketing plan which allows accessibility features in rental housing to be adjusted to suit the needs of both disabled and non-disabled tenants. When the unit is rented to non-disabled people, fixtures can be placed in conventional positions or be omitted. These same fixtures and features can be quickly and inexpensively adjusted to better meet the needs of disabled tenants when they occupy the units. In adaptable dwelling units, the counter segments can be set at multiple heights and the knee spaces can either be left clear or occupied by removable base cabinets or storage carts that can be relocated as needed.

The adaptable design concept helps to eliminate the "special look" of accessible dwellings thus making them more marketable. For more detail on adaptable housing design, the reader is referred to the Housing and Urban Development publication titled *Adaptable Housing: A Technical Manual for Implementing the Adaptable Dwelling Unit Specifications.* The manual provides information which is in accord with the ANSI and UFAS standards.

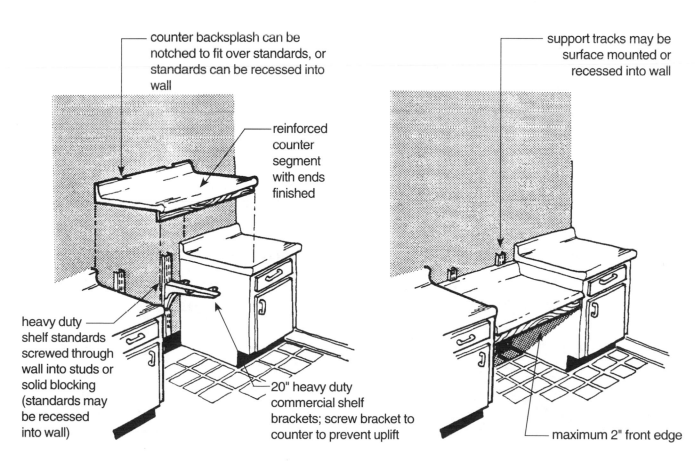

Wall-mounted, Adjustable Support Brackets

counter backsplash can be notched to fit over standards, or standards can be recessed into wall

reinforced counter segment with ends finished

heavy duty shelf standards screwed through wall into studs or solid blocking (standards may be recessed into wall)

20" heavy duty commercial shelf brackets; screw bracket to counter to prevent uplift

Lowered Counter on Wall-mounted, Adjustable Support Brackets

support tracks may be surface mounted or recessed into wall

maximum 2" front edge

Cabinets and Storage

Much of conventional kitchen cabinet storage space is not useable by disabled individuals because of limited reach ranges, an inability to bend over, lift heavy objects with one hand, or climb up on step stools or chairs. These limitations, combined with the need to omit some base cabinets to create knee spaces, can result in accessible kitchens with inadequate storage capacity. Most of the unusable space can be recovered or replaced by installing more efficient and accessible storage in the space that is available.

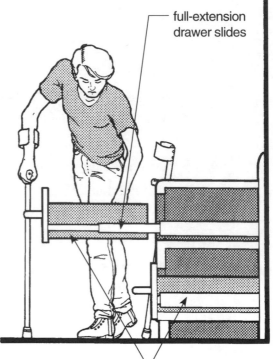

full-extension
drawer slides

file type full
depth drawers
for bulk storage

Cabinets and Storage

Full-extension Drawers

Drawers that are deep, extend the full depth of the base cabinets, and are mounted on full-extension slides make the best use of available storage space. When fully extended, these drawers display their entire contents and place them within easy reach.

Banks of full-extension drawers can make the total volume of base cabinet space accessible to most users. Drawers can be of any size and proportion to suit the contents. Such drawers can be used for storing pots and pans, bowls, kitchen utensils, dry food, or small appliances.

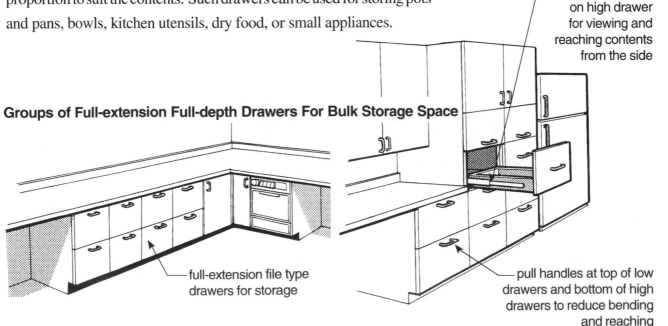

Groups of Full-extension Full-depth Drawers For Bulk Storage Space

full-extension file type
drawers for storage

low drawer sides
on high drawer
for viewing and
reaching contents
from the side

pull handles at top of low
drawers and bottom of high
drawers to reduce bending
and reaching

Low Drawer Sides for
Viewing and Reaching Contents

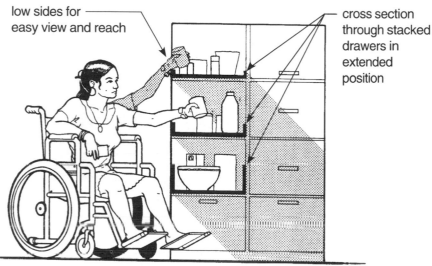

low sides for easy view and reach

cross section through stacked drawers in extended position

Typical Full-Extension Drawer With Low Side

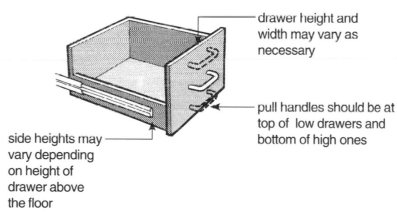

drawer height and width may vary as necessary

pull handles should be at top of low drawers and bottom of high ones

side heights may vary depending on height of drawer above the floor

Cabinets and Storage
Full-extension Drawers

Full-extension drawers can be stacked up to 5'-0" above the floor to create a storage wall. One or both sides of drawers can be low to make the contents easier to see and reach. When stacked, high drawers should have lower sides to facilitate access; and low drawers, which tend to be deeper and easier to reach, may have higher sides. This type of full-extension drawer may have to be custom built or specially ordered from cabinet suppliers.

Several cabinet and accessory manufacturers make drawers and devices such as rotating or sliding cabinet shelves that can be installed in existing cabinets. These devices are readily available and are more accessible than conventional fixed shelving but will not provide the same storage volume as those described above.

Two Types of Manufactured Accessible Base Cabinet Units

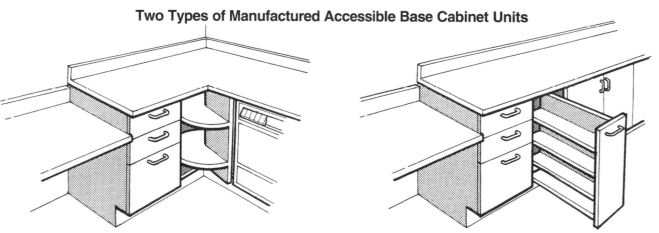

Cabinets and Storage
Carts

Rolling carts designed to fit into knee spaces under countertops can provide additional storage space. Such carts can be easily rolled out when the knee space is needed. The tops of these carts can also provide additional convenient work space and a safe method for transporting food and utensils from the counter to the table.

Movable Carts as Storage and a Method of Transporting Items

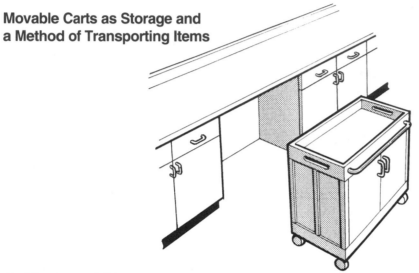

rolling carts provide movable storage that can be placed in a knee space or be moved out when the space is needed

Cabinets and Storage
Countertop Storage Unit

The space between countertops and the bottom of wall cabinets can provide useful, easily reached open storage. This space can be utilized by installing countertop storage shelves, appliance garages, or storage devices designed to hang on the bottom of wall cabinets.

Countertop Storage Units Are Within Comfortable Reach Ranges

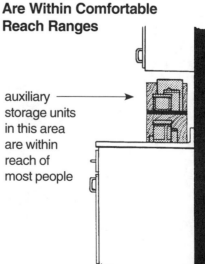

auxiliary storage units in this area are within reach of most people

A Free-standing Countertop Shelf Unit

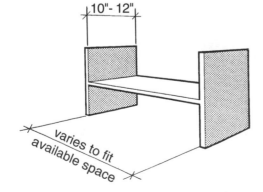

10"- 12"

varies to fit available space

Cabinets and Storage
Overhead Cabinet Doors

When left standing open, swinging wall cabinet doors can become a hazard for blind people. Hardware that allows cabinet doors to swing up and stay open, rather than swing out, eliminates the problem of protruding doors for blind people and provide full view of cabinet contents for others.

Overhead Cabinet Doors

protruding doors can be a hazard for blind people

swing-up cabinet door hardware increases headroom and safety for some standing users

Cabinets and Storage
Concealing Knee Space

Swinging retractable cabinet door hardware can make it possible to conceal knee spaces. This special hardware allows the doors to be opened in the traditional manner and then if desired, the doors can be pushed back under the counter out of the way.

Concealing Knee Space

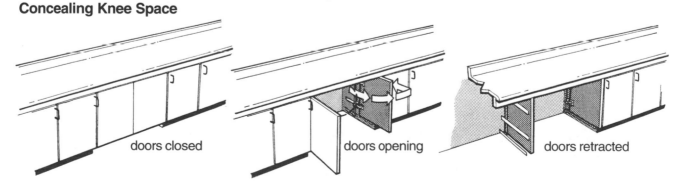

doors closed | doors opening | doors retracted

Ranges

Ranges have some inherent features that make them less than ideal for all users. Ranges almost always have cooking surfaces 35"-36" above the floor. These heights are comfortable for average size standing people including mobility impaired people who use walkers, canes, or crutches. However, 35"-36" is not a particularly good height for seated or very short people because they will have difficulty reaching back burners and will generally not be able to see food cooking in pots on these burners.

With the exception of drop-in models, ranges cannot be installed with their cooking surfaces at anything but the conventional manufactured height of 35" or 36". When ranges are used, seated and very short people may have to cope with the awkward height and/or make special adaptations to assist them with cooking. Cooktops, which can be installed at almost any height, offer an alternative to ranges (see "Cooktops" below).

Ranges cannot have knee space directly underneath the cooking surface. Access for seated users is therefore limited to parallel approach, which in turn necessitates a sideways reach to the controls and burners. These constraints further complicate cooking for seated users.

Ranges are an economical and commonly used cooking appliance. Despite their disadvantages to some users they must be included in planning for accessible kitchens. Careful selection and placement of ranges can mitigate some of their difficulties and make them more universally useable.

Rear-mounted Controls are Dangerous for Everyone and Should Be Avoided

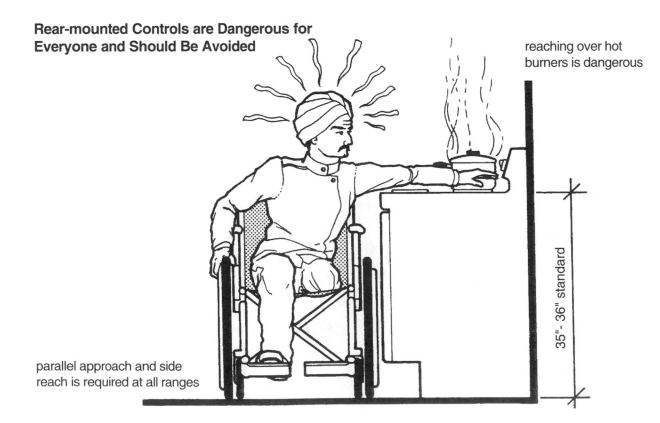

reaching over hot burners is dangerous

35" - 36" standard

parallel approach and side reach is required at all ranges

Ranges

Placement of Controls

One feature of ranges which has a great effect on safety and usability for everyone is the location of the controls. Ranges with controls at the rear should not be used. Controls which are placed at the back of the rangetop behind the burners are difficult and dangerous for everyone. This control location increases the chance of burning oneself while reaching across heated surfaces. This design is extremely dangerous for seated and short people and for others who have limited balance, arm and hand strength, or limited sight.

Ranges with controls on or near the front eliminate the need to reach over or between hot burners and steaming pots to adjust the temperature. This placement also allows those with limited sight to get close enough to see the controls.

Range hood controls should be located on the lower front panel of the hood to reduce the reach distance required to operate them. It is preferable that stove hood controls be located on the stove control panel or in the face panel of nearby base cabinets just below the countertop.

Standard Ranges Do Not Work Well for Short People

rear-mounted controls

reaching over pans of cooking food is dangerous

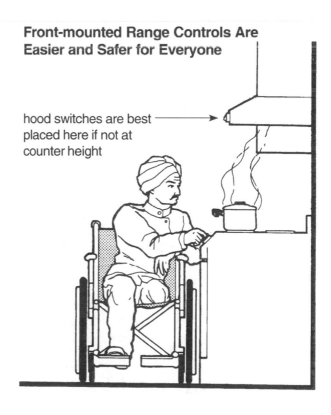

Front-mounted Range Controls Are Easier and Safer for Everyone

hood switches are best placed here if not at counter height

Ovens in Ranges

Ovens in ranges are usually quite low and may be difficult for mobility impaired standing people to use. For a variety of reasons, these people frequently have limited ability to bend over and reach with both hands to lift items in or out of the oven. For these users, a wall oven or a countertop oven appliance may be a better choice.

For wheelchair users, the range oven may be difficult to use because the drop-front door gets in the way of maneuvering one's chair close to the oven racks thus restricting reach into the oven. A knee space installed beside a conventional range allows wheelchair users to pull in close enough to use the oven with one hand. This space also helps wheelchair users reach burners and manipulate pots. When designing a kitchen for a particular individual, the knee space should be placed on the side of the range that is best for their use.

It is also best for mobility impaired users to have at least 12" of clear counter space on each side of a range. This provides a location where hot pots and pans can be temporarily placed after they are removed from burners or ovens.

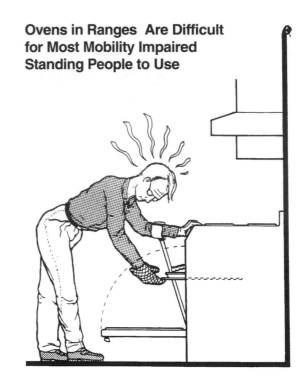

Ovens in Ranges Are Difficult for Most Mobility Impaired Standing People to Use

A Knee Space Beside a Range Can Improve Use of the Range by a Wheelchair User

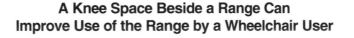

minimum 12" of counter space on each side of range at level of cooking surface is preferred

Wall Ovens

Some people cannot use ovens in ranges because they are unable to bend and lift pans in and out or because the door prevents close approach to the oven and requires reaching and lifting with one hand. Most people can use wall ovens if they are installed in a manner that minimizes the need to lift or carry hot pots.

Wall Ovens

Drop-front Wall Ovens

Drop-front ovens can be made more useable by installing them so that one oven rack is at the level of the adjacent countertop. This installation provides a shorter transfer distance for pans as they are moved from the extended oven rack to the counter. A pullout shelf, installed next to the oven, just below the counter top, and at the same height as the oven rack would also serve to reduce the need to lift and carry heavy pans from the oven to the counter. For wheelchair users, a knee space should be provided on at least one side of the oven to allow a closer approach.

Drop-front Oven with Rack at Counter Height and Knee Space on One Side

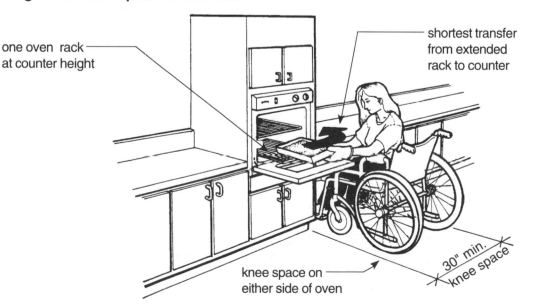

one oven rack at counter height

shortest transfer from extended rack to counter

knee space on either side of oven

30" min. knee space

Wall Ovens

Side-hinged, Swinging Door, Wall and Countertop Ovens

Side-hinged oven doors are best for many people because they allow the user to get closer to the oven and thus require less reaching or bending while moving hot pans. Because of product safety regulations, ovens with side-hinged doors may only be available in microwave or convection models.

Ovens with side-hinged doors may be installed at countertop level and should have a shelf below. The shelf should be approximately 10" wide and extend the full width of the oven or greater. This shelf can be either a permanent shelf, such as the front edge of the counter, or a pullout shelf, installed just under the

countertop, that can be used when needed for transferring hot pans. There should also be a knee space either under the oven or beside the oven on the side closest to the door handle, to facilitate use by wheelchair users.

The oven with swinging door, placed in a corner at a 45 degree angle with knee space below, allows the 10" minimum shelf to connect both adjacent counters. This position eliminates most lifting, allows containers to be slid past the wall oven (see "Food Flow Kitchen" later in this section), and places counter space within reach of users without their having to move about.

Corner-mounted Oven with Side-swinging Door and Continuous Countertop Shelf

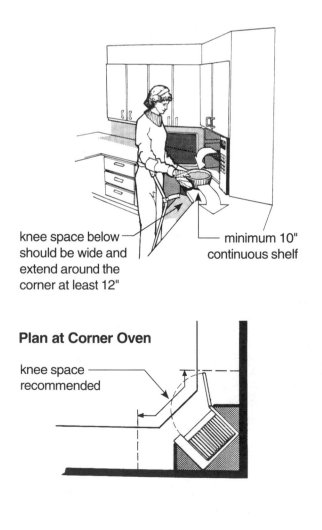

knee space below should be wide and extend around the corner at least 12"

minimum 10" continuous shelf

Oven with Swinging Door and Pullout Shelf Below

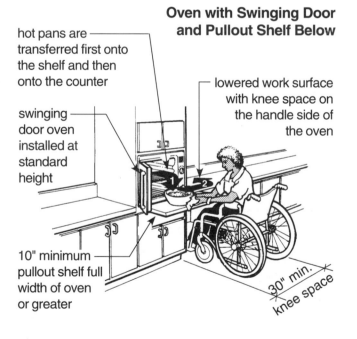

hot pans are transferred first onto the shelf and then onto the counter

swinging door oven installed at standard height

lowered work surface with knee space on the handle side of the oven

10" minimum pullout shelf full width of oven or greater

30" min. knee space

Plan at Corner Oven

knee space recommended

Extended Width Pullout Shelf at Oven

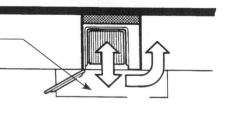

pullout shelf wider than oven allows hot pans to be moved with a minimum of lifting

Cooktops

Countertop cooktop units are a good choice for many mobility impaired people who have difficulty using ranges. They are particularly useful for short or seated people because they can be placed in low counter segments and can be installed with knee spaces below.

Cooktops can be installed in fixed countertops located at any height above the floor. They can also be installed in adjustable height counters that can be set to the most convenient height for the user. Adjustable height cooktops must have flexible electrical or gas supply lines.

As described earlier in the section on "Counter Heights", adjustments in the height of cooktops can be either manual or motor driven. Manually adjusted cooktops are most useful in rental housing where there is likely to be a turnover of tenants with different preferences. The more expensive, motor driven, adjustable height cooktops are used most often in homes where both seated or short people and standing people are likely to use the kitchen frequently.

The sheet metal underside of cooktop units can get hot during use. When installed with knee spaces below, the exposed underside may need to be enclosed and insulated to prevent people from touching the hot surfaces.

If knee space is provided under cooktop units, it should be at least 30" wide. It is best if knee spaces extend the full depth of the counter but they must extend at least 19" under the front edge of the countertop. The height of the knee space will depend upon the thickness of the cooking unit, the counter structure, and the height it is set above the floor. It is best to keep the counter and cooking unit as thin as possible to provide the greatest possible knee space height for any counter position.

Cooktop with Knee Space Below

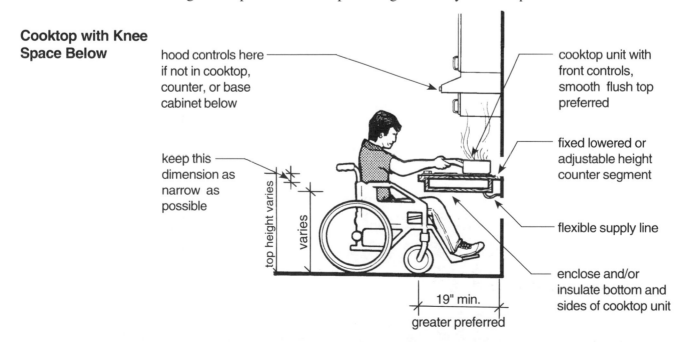

hood controls here if not in cooktop, counter, or base cabinet below

keep this dimension as narrow as possible

top height varies

varies

19" min.
greater preferred

cooktop unit with front controls, smooth flush top preferred

fixed lowered or adjustable height counter segment

flexible supply line

enclose and/or insulate bottom and sides of cooktop unit

Cooktops

Special Configurations

Cooktop units can be useful in meeting the special needs of particular individuals with disabilities because they offer a degree of flexibility not possible with ranges. For example, two burner cooktop units might be mounted parallel to cabinets for people who cannot reach back burners on conventional units. Two burner units might also be installed at different levels in households where both standing and seated users wish to cook.

Parallel Arrangement for Easy Reach to All Burners

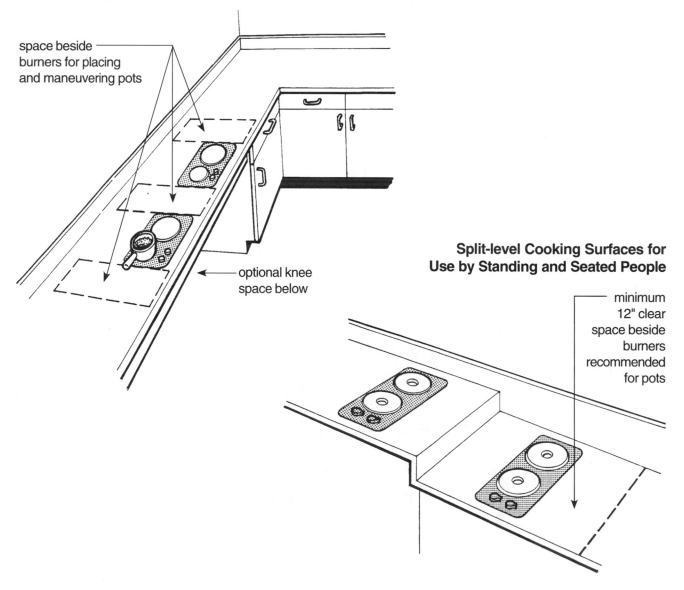

space beside burners for placing and maneuvering pots

optional knee space below

Split-level Cooking Surfaces for Use by Standing and Seated People

minimum 12" clear space beside burners recommended for pots

Designers, Owners, and Users Must Exercise Great Care in the Design and Use of Kitchens

wheelchair users are at greater risk of spilling pots at ranges with rear controls

Some Suggested Features to Improve Safety of Cooktops

12"   12"

minimum 12" clear counter space at same level on each side for pots

sink spray hose reaches some burners so water can be added to hot pots to cool them

burners, cooktop, and counters at a smooth common level - no more than 1/8" raised edge

A Note On Cooking Safety

Cooking is a hazardous task for everyone because of the intense heat utilized, the risk of spilling boiling food, and splashing hot grease or oil. Everyone must be careful when confronting these hazardous elements. Mobility impaired people may have more difficulty cooking and may need to exercise even greater care. Seated people must be extremely careful because they may be at greater risk than others due to their inability to move quickly. Features such as lowered cooking surfaces, knee spaces, and controls located at the front make cooking easier and therefore safer for mobility impaired people.

Knee spaces allow close approach that permits some wheelchair users to cook who otherwise could not. However, this close approach places users in closer proximity to heat sources and increases the obvious potential of spilling boiling food into their laps while sitting under a cooktop. Recognizing that hot food can be spilled into one's lap from a range as well, it seems clear that safety concerns should not preclude the installation of accessible cooking facilities of either type.

Designers, owners, and users must weigh the relative risks against independent usability and exercise care in the design and use of kitchens. Cooking safety can be achieved in properly designed kitchens using techniques taught by rehabilitation and occupational therapy specialists. For example, one can reduce or eliminate the most dangerous step of moving a pot of hot food on or off raised burners by reducing heat early in the cooking process and by adding a small amount of cold water or other liquid to further reduce temperatures before moving the pot from the burner. Designers can facilitate this process by installing the cooking unit close to a sink and including a sink spray hose that can reach some burners. Units with flush burners should be specified so full pots can be slid from stove to counter without being lifted.

These and other safety features suggested by design specialists and therapists may be necessary in kitchens designed for users with specific disabilities. Some features may be less appropriate for open market rental housing but many ideas can be incorporated into products and buildings to improve safety and use for all residents.

Kitchen Sinks

Sinks for use by seated people should be relatively shallow and should have the drain located as far to the rear as possible so the plumbing connections and piping do not encroach on the knee space needed below.

Sinks for use by seated people can be installed in standard height or lowered countertops but, in either case, should have knee spaces below. The height of clear knee spaces under sinks may be impossible to maintain due to the depth of the front panel required to cover the sink basin. However, the maximum possible height of clear knee space should always be provided.

Sinks should be mounted in the counter as close to the front as possible to facilitate reach to controls. Plumbing below the sink should be covered by a removable sloping protection/appearance panel to prevent skin contact with hot or sharp surfaces.

Kitchen Sinks

Corner Locations for Sinks

Sinks located in corners at a 45 degree angle to adjacent cabinets, provide countertop space that can be reached on both sides of the sink without the user having to move back and forth. The required knee space uses corner space which is usually allocated to inefficient storage. For some mobility impaired people, this location may provide some significant advantages.

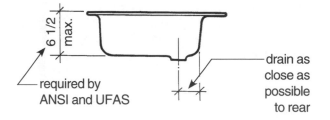

Sink Section

6 1/2 max.

required by ANSI and UFAS

drain as close as possible to rear

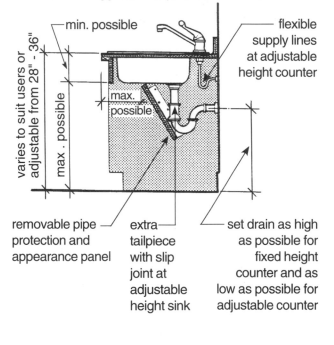

Section at Typical Accessible Kitchen Sink

min. possible

flexible supply lines at adjustable height counter

varies to suit users or adjustable from 28" - 36"

max. possible

max. possible

removable pipe protection and appearance panel

extra tailpiece with slip joint at adjustable height sink

set drain as high as possible for fixed height counter and as low as possible for adjustable counter

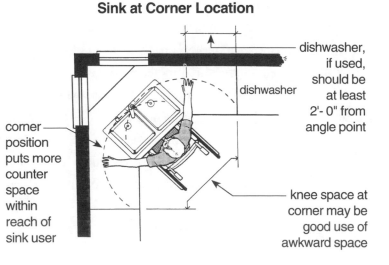

Sink at Corner Location

dishwasher, if used, should be at least 2'- 0" from angle point

dishwasher

corner position puts more counter space within reach of sink user

knee space at corner may be good use of awkward space

Kitchen Sinks

Disposals at Sinks

Because of their size and installation requirements, disposals may not fit behind the protection/appearance panels suggested above and therefore may interfere with knee spaces. When a disposal will not fit behind the panel and a double bowl sink is used, the disposal can be installed under one bowl and enclosed in a full depth base cabinet. In this situation, it is best if a wide knee space is provided to give access to an adjacent counter space or work surface.

Section at Enclosed Disposal

Enclosed Disposal and Knee Space at Lower Sink

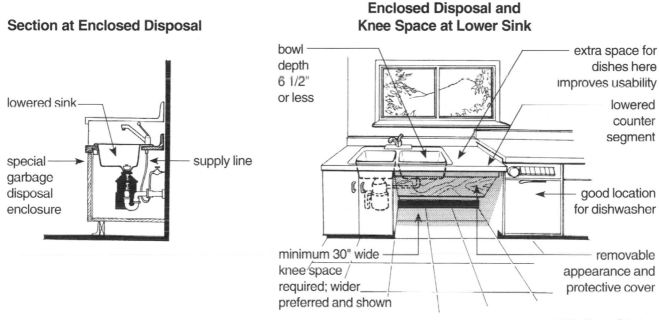

lowered sink

special garbage disposal enclosure

supply line

bowl depth 6 1/2" or less

extra space for dishes here improves usability

lowered counter segment

good location for dishwasher

minimum 30" wide knee space required; wider preferred and shown

removable appearance and protective cover

Knee Space Beside Dishwasher

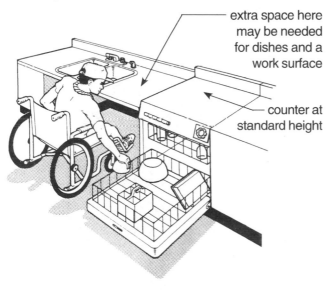

extra space here may be needed for dishes and a work surface

counter at standard height

Kitchen Sinks

Dishwashers at Sinks

Standard dishwashers with drop-front doors, roll-out baskets and front controls seem to be adequate for most users. A knee space should be provided beside a dishwasher to accommodate seated users. The knee space can usually be the same one provided under sinks.

Counter heights over dishwashers must be at the standard 36" height. If lowered or adjustable height sinks are planned, extra space and care in locating the dishwasher may be necessary so the change in height doesn't make use of the sink inconvenient.

Side-by-side Refrigerator

side-by-side refrigerator provides spaces at all reach levels

Top Freezer Refrigerator

50% of the freezer volume should be within reach of a seated person

4'- 0" max. preferred

plan

counter space each side is preferred

2'- 6" x 4'- 0" clear floor spaces for parallel approach

plan

counter space

locate refrigerator away from corners so door can be opened to a 180 degree position

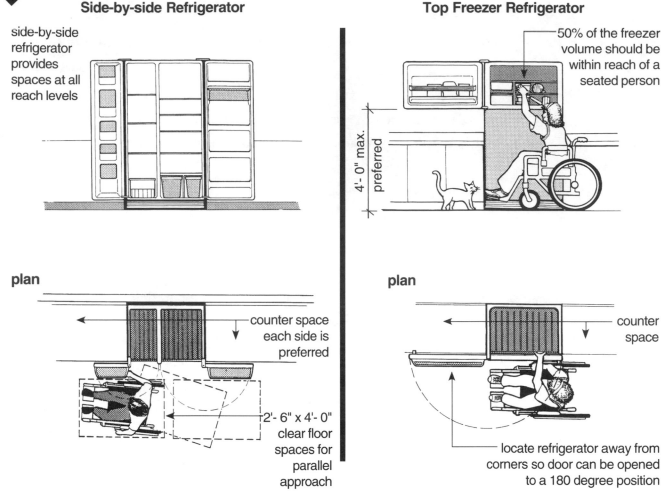

Refrigerators

Both top freezer and side freezer models of refrigerators are acceptable for accessible kitchens if they are carefully selected and installed. Side-by-side refrigerator/freezers provide the greatest access for seated and short people because both freezer and refrigerated space is available at all reach heights. Top freezer models work for people who are able to reach as high as 4'- 6". In top freezer models, at least one half of freezer space should be below 4'- 6" and it is best if the bottom of the top freezer is 4'- 0" or less above the floor.

Both types should be located away from a corner so the doors can be opened the full 180 degrees. This placement allows parallel approach and provides easy access to door racks for wheelchair users.

Through-the-door ice and water dispensers can be a great convenience for many mobility impaired people, particularly those who have hand limitations which make ice tray use impossible.

Ice and Water Dispensers May Be a Necessity for Many Mobility Impaired People

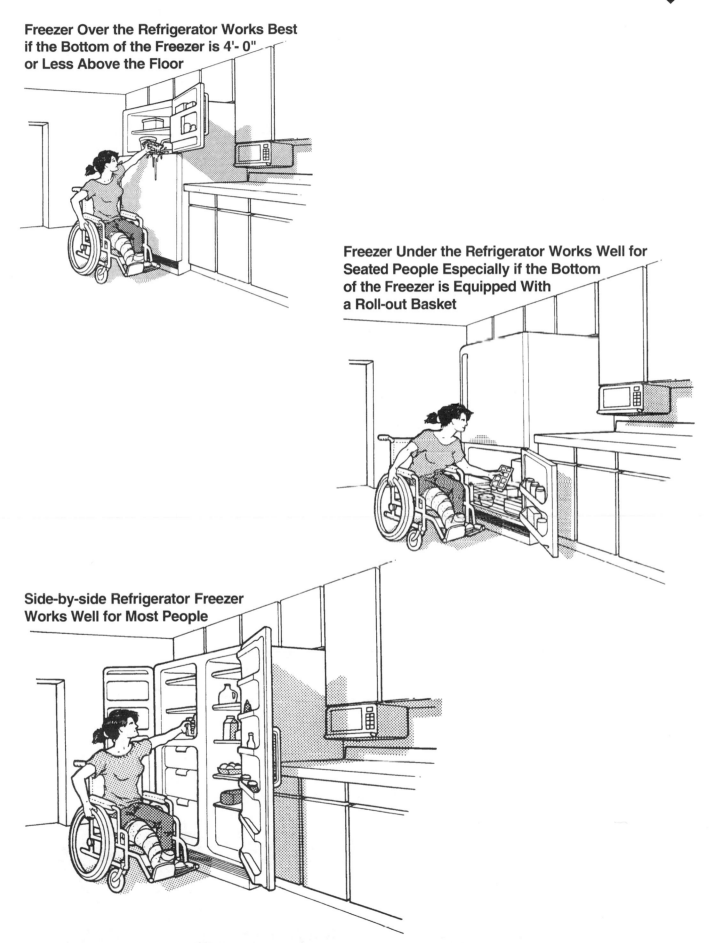

Freezer Over the Refrigerator Works Best if the Bottom of the Freezer is 4'- 0" or Less Above the Floor

Freezer Under the Refrigerator Works Well for Seated People Especially if the Bottom of the Freezer is Equipped With a Roll-out Basket

Side-by-side Refrigerator Freezer Works Well for Most People

Controls and Handles

People who have limited use of their hands and people who have limited or no sight may have difficulty using some very common controls. For example, smooth round knobs are difficult to both grip and twist and it is impossible to know where they are set unless you can see to read some surface graphics or words. Such controls should be avoided.

Lever-type controls are ideal because they do not require grasping to operate and their shape provides a natural pointer to indicate the control's position. However, lever handles on appliances are rare. The next best common choice is a control with a large straight blade across the center that is used both to turn the knob and to indicate its position. Blade knobs are better if the blade position is asymmetrical so it extends on one side to form a more distinct pointer. This shape also serves as a small lever providing mechanical advantage and allowing it to be turned with little effort.

Poor Choice

smooth round knobs are difficult for people with hand limitations as well as for people with visual impairments

Better Control Choices

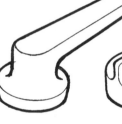

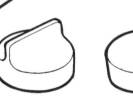

levers are ideal but rarely found on appliances

blades help indicate position and make turning somewhat easier

small lever or extended blade provides position pointer and leverage for easy turning without gripping

Lever handles are available for faucets at sinks and they are a good choice for all users. These handles are available in a wide variety of styles and colors to suit almost any decor.

lever handles on faucets are easy for most people to operate

The ANSI and UFAS design standards give a performance specification for controls that essentially states they must be operable with one hand, not require gripping or twisting nor more than 5 lbs. of force to operate. A simple and useful test for this is to attempt to operate any control in question with a closed fist. If it can be operated with a closed fist and little effort, it probably complies. Lever handles, push plates, touch surfaces, and asymmetrical shapes usually work well.

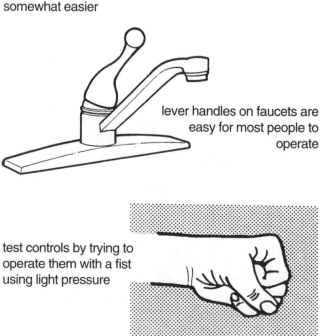

test controls by trying to operate them with a fist using light pressure

Controls and Handles
Redundant Cuing In Controls

In addition to being easy for people with limited strength to manipulate, controls should provide redundant cuing or feedback to facilitate use by people with visual and hearing impairments.

For example, a lever or other asymmetrical handle equipped with a pointer gives instant visual or tactile feedback about its position. This shape used in combination with click stops creates a control mechanism which is safer for all users. The click stops should be located at important increments and provide a distinct audible sound and tactile cue that can be detected by anyone.

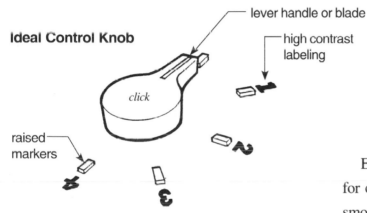

Ideal Control Knob

lever handle or blade

high contrast labeling

click

raised markers

Controls and Handles
Electric Touch Controls

Electric and touch sensitive controls meet the test for operable controls. However, since they have a smooth printed surface, they are not useful for people with visual impairments who may have difficulty knowing which spot to touch. Some manufacturers have begun offering plastic overlay panels that have raised tactile openings or labeling that can help visually impaired people.

Smooth Electronic Touch Pad Controls Are Easy For People With Hand Limitations To Operate

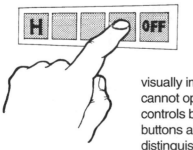

visually impaired people cannot operate these controls because the buttons are not distinguishable by touch

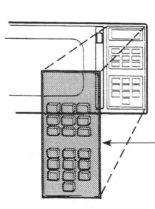

Add-on Tactile Panel For Visually Impaired People

plastic overlay panel

Controls and Handles

Adapting Difficult Controls

Appliance controls that require pressing while turning may be impossible to operate for some people with limited strength or hand dexterity. In some cases, it may be possible to weaken the internal springs to require less force. Care must be exercised not to eliminate the click stops which help prevent accidental turning of the control.

Some simple electric controls, such as range hood switches, that may be too high or out of reach can be bypassed by installing a conventional switch that is used as an auxiliary control. The hood switchs are set and left on so the conveniently located new switch can be used for on and off switching.

Controls That Must Be Pushed Down and Then Turned Are Difficult For Many People To Use

internal springs sometimes can be weakened to make turning easier

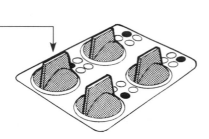

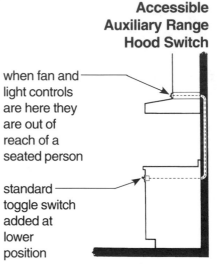

when fan and light controls are here they are out of reach of a seated person

standard toggle switch added at lower position

Controls and Handles

Light Switches and Other Controls

Rocker switches, toggle switches, and touch type electronic switches are good choices because they can be operated by a single touch, require little force, and do not require gripping, twisting, or fine finger dexterity.

Switches Most People Can Operate

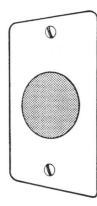

touch sensitive

toggle

rocker

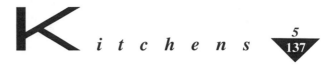
Controls and Handles

Suggested Switch Location for Easy Reach

Switches for lights, exhaust fans, disposal units, and motorized countertops are within reach of all users when installed at the front near the top of the base cabinets. This is also a recommended and convenient location for several electrical receptacles.

Suggested Alternative Switch Placement

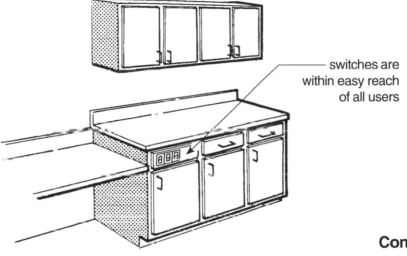

switches are
within easy reach
of all users

Controls and Handles

Handles

Drawer and door handles that do not require gripping or twisting are needed for people who have limited hand strength.

Loop handles, that allow the user to put their hands or fingers through the loop, do not require gripping and can be used by most people. Handles with at least a 4" by 1-1/2" clear space are good choices.

Handles on base cabinet doors should be mounted as high as possible and on wall cabinets as low as possible.

Loop Handles Are Easiest To Use

**Best Locations
for Cabinet Handles**

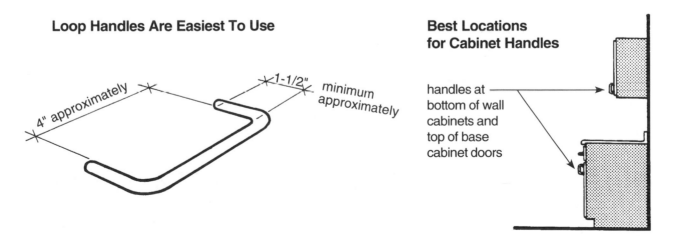

4" approximately   1-1/2" minimum approximately

handles at
bottom of wall
cabinets and
top of base
cabinet doors

Three Examples of Accessible Kitchens

Following are three sample kitchens that incorporate many of the access features discussed earlier. The first is a small U-shaped kitchen that better meets the needs of severely mobility impaired people, such as a person who uses a wheelchair and has limited use of their arms and hands. The second is also a small U-shaped kitchen, but it would be more appropriate for someone who is less severely disabled. The last is a more spacious kitchen that exceeds the minimum requirements in the accessibility standards and includes many suggested features. In addition to the kitchen configurations shown here, numerous other spatial arrangements are possible.

Food Flow Diagram

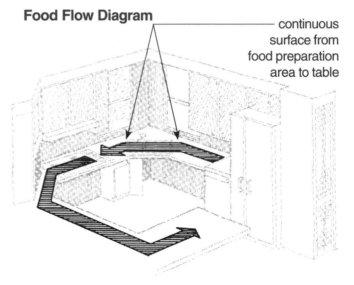

continuous surface from food preparation area to table

Example One

Small Kitchen Incorporating Food Flow Concept

Some severely disabled people are unable to pick up a bowl or pot full of food and carry it across a room while at the same time maneuvering their crutches, wheelchair, or other support device. The kitchen shown here is arranged in an extended U-shaped plan. The sequence of the work areas and appliances is designed to facilitate food preparation. All counters and surfaces provide a continuous, common level surface from food preparation area to the table. Food containers and other items can remain on the counter surface while being moved from place to place and onto the table.

this kitchen works well for a severely mobility impaired person who might have difficulty lifting heavy pots and pans

Small Kitchen Incorporating Food Flow Concept

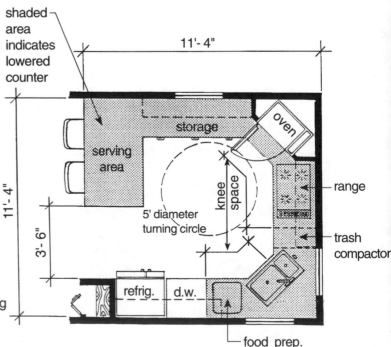

shaded area indicates lowered counter

serving area

storage

oven

range

trash compactor

5' diameter turning circle

knee space

11'- 4"

11'- 4"

3'- 6"

refrig.

d.w.

food prep.

Small Kitchen Incorporating Food Flow Concept

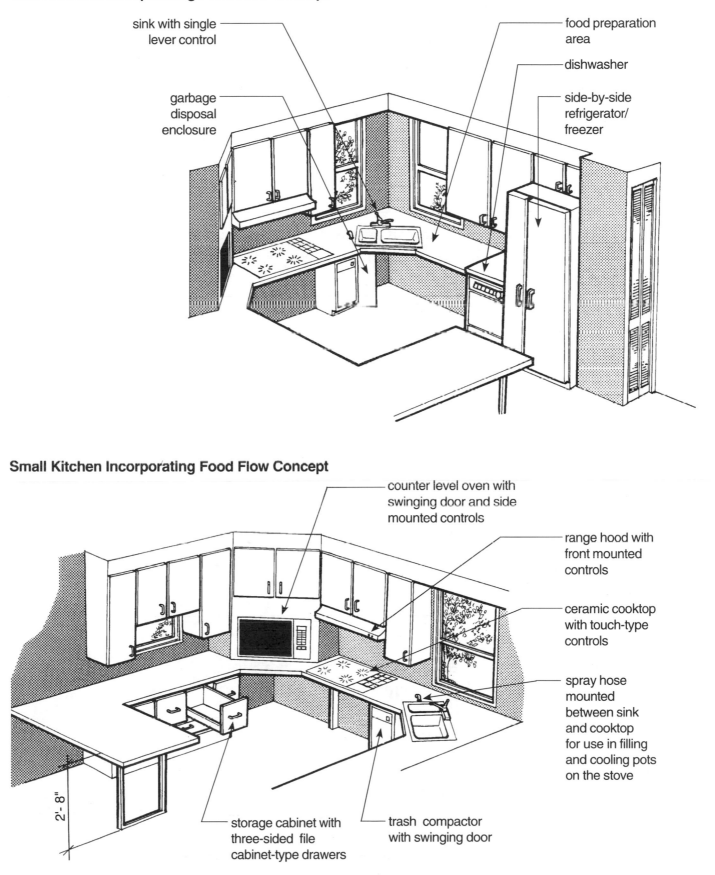

sink with single lever control

food preparation area

dishwasher

garbage disposal enclosure

side-by-side refrigerator/ freezer

Small Kitchen Incorporating Food Flow Concept

counter level oven with swinging door and side mounted controls

range hood with front mounted controls

ceramic cooktop with touch-type controls

spray hose mounted between sink and cooktop for use in filling and cooling pots on the stove

2'- 8"

storage cabinet with three-sided file cabinet-type drawers

trash compactor with swinging door

Example Two
Small U-Shaped Kitchen

In this kitchen, the user may be required to carry and lift dishes or full pots and pans across the kitchen. As in the first kitchen, heavy pots or dishes can be slid along some sections of the counter to their desired location. However, cooking is not as convenient. A range (included in this kitchen design) is generally not as easy for seated people to use as a cooktop. However, with the placement of knee space beside the range, the appliance's usability for wheelchair users is greatly improved. The user can pull up beside the range and reach into pots on the burners as well as into the oven.

The knee space beside the range provides a space to store a movable cart when the range is not in use. The cart shown in this plan adds an element of flexibility and convenience to the kitchen. For wheelchair users who may not be able to carry plates or hot items in their lap while they push or operate their chair, the cart can be used as a serving tray to transport items to the eating area. The cart top can double as an auxiliary lowered food preparation area while the interior of the cart can serve as additional storage space.

Plan of a Small U-Shaped Kitchen

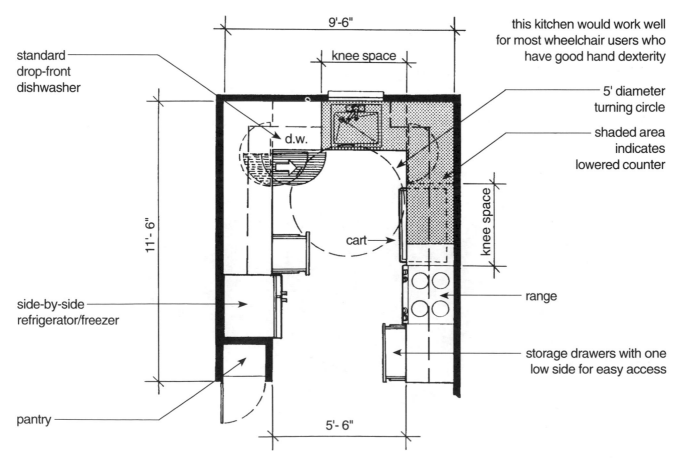

standard drop-front dishwasher

knee space

9'-6"

this kitchen would work well for most wheelchair users who have good hand dexterity

5' diameter turning circle

shaded area indicates lowered counter

d.w.

11'- 6"

cart

knee space

side-by-side refrigerator/freezer

range

storage drawers with one low side for easy access

pantry

5'- 6"

Small U-Shaped Kitchen

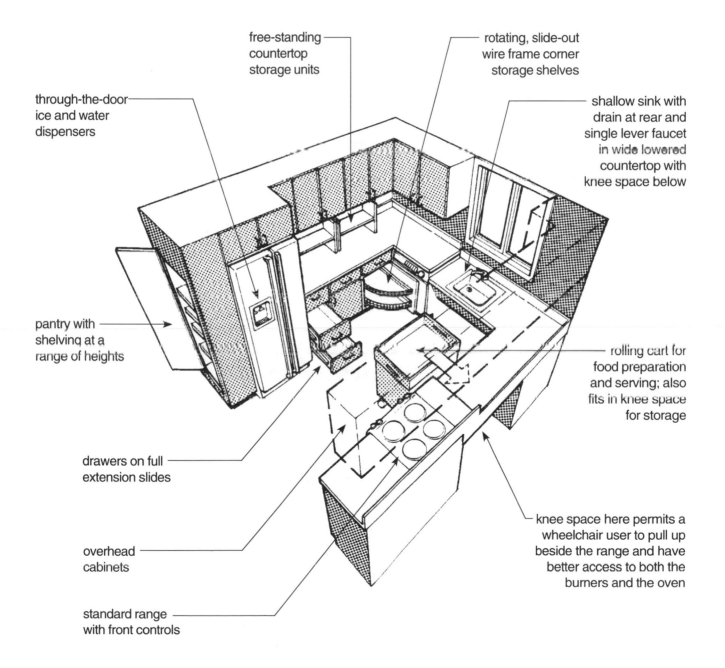

free-standing countertop storage units

rotating, slide-out wire frame corner storage shelves

through-the-door ice and water dispensers

shallow sink with drain at rear and single lever faucet in wide lowered countertop with knee space below

pantry with shelving at a range of heights

rolling cart for food preparation and serving; also fits in knee space for storage

drawers on full extension slides

overhead cabinets

knee space here permits a wheelchair user to pull up beside the range and have better access to both the burners and the oven

standard range with front controls

Example Three

Spacious Kitchen With Eat-in Area

Despite the base cabinet area that is devoted to knee space, this kitchen has a significant amount of accessible storage space. The lazy Susan in the corner between the cooktop and the sink, the pantry, the cabinets in the corner beside the refrigerator, and the bank of storage drawers gives this kitchen an ample amount of storage that both standing and seated mobility impaired people can use.

Most of the major kitchen activities such as cleaning, food preparation, and cooking can be performed at a lowered counter. The knee space below the cooktop allows a seated person to get close enough to the oven to safely place full dishes into and remove hot dishes from the oven. The refrigerator is somewhat removed from the washing/cooking area but it is still within the appropriate distance for an accessible kitchen. The kitchen eating area doubles as an additional lowered work area, permitting more than one disabled person to be in the kitchen assisting with meal preparation.

Plan of a Spacious Kitchen With Eat-in Area

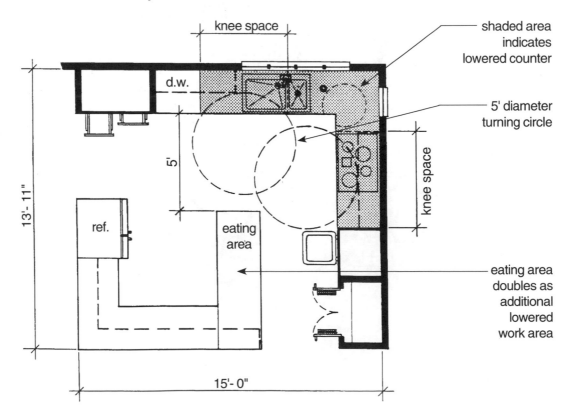

Spacious Kitchen With Eat-in Area

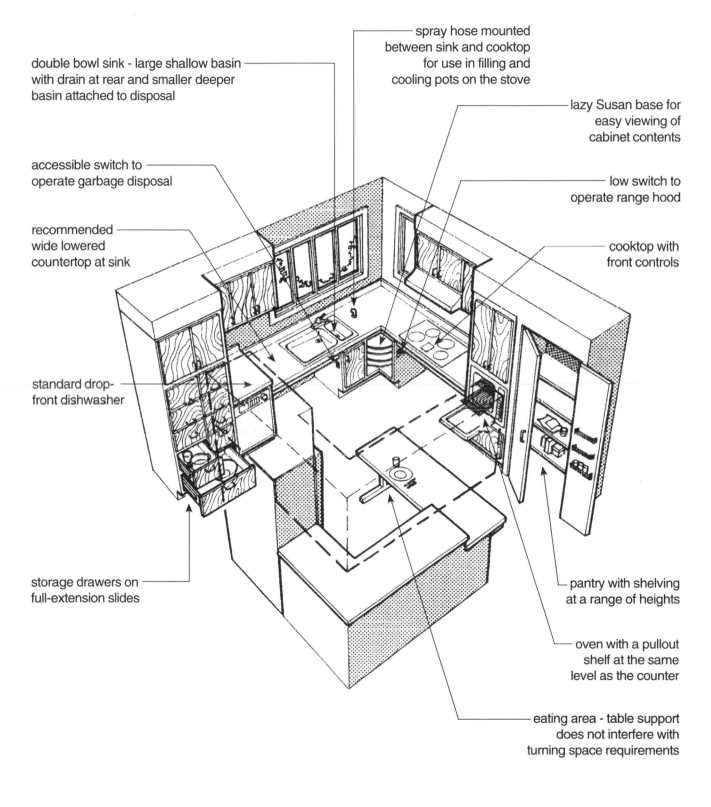

double bowl sink - large shallow basin with drain at rear and smaller deeper basin attached to disposal

spray hose mounted between sink and cooktop for use in filling and cooling pots on the stove

lazy Susan base for easy viewing of cabinet contents

accessible switch to operate garbage disposal

low switch to operate range hood

recommended wide lowered countertop at sink

cooktop with front controls

standard drop-front dishwasher

pantry with shelving at a range of heights

storage drawers on full-extension slides

oven with a pullout shelf at the same level as the counter

eating area - table support does not interfere with turning space requirements

B *a t h r o o m s*  145

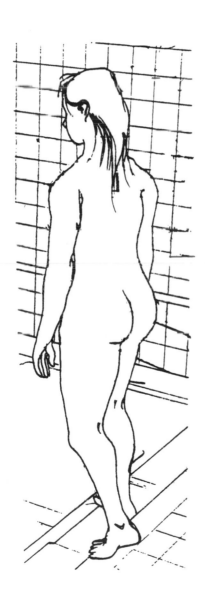

continued on next page

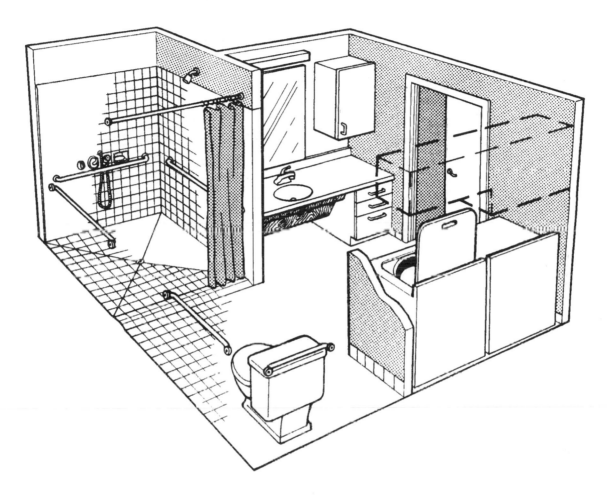

Accessible Bathrooms

To be used independently by mobility impaired people (those who use wheelchairs, walkers, crutches, or canes), bathrooms need not be particularly large, but must be carefully designed. Attention must be given to what type of bathing fixture is preferred by the potential user: a tub, a transfer shower, or a roll-in shower. In addition, careful planning must be done to provide critical clear floor space at each fixture so someone with a mobility aid can approach, maneuver close to, and use all fixtures. Knee space at lavatories (sinks), faucets and controls, as well as grab bar size and position must be considered.

Tub with Removable Seat

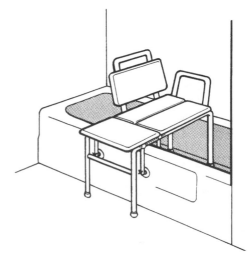

Tub with Built-in Transfer Seat

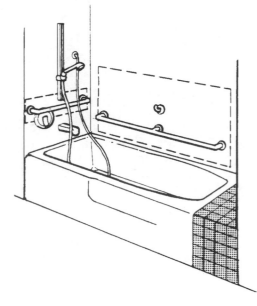

Bathing

Three types of bathing fixtures are commonly used by people with mobility impairments: 1) a standard bathtub with a built-in transfer surface or a removable seat, 2) a special 3' wide by 3' deep transfer shower stall with a corner seat, and 3) a roll-in shower stall (with no curb) that is large enough to permit people to shower in a wheelchair. Each of these three bathing fixtures has advantages and disadvantages that make them more suitable for some people and less suitable for others. Since no one fixture meets everyone's needs, the following sections present each of the fixtures, explain their key features and how they are used.

3' x 3' Transfer Shower

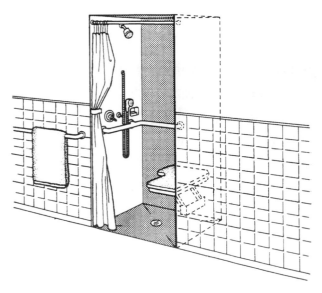

5' x 5' Roll-in Shower

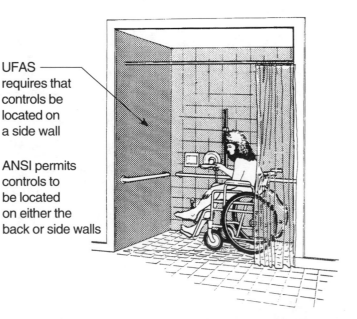

UFAS requires that controls be located on a side wall

ANSI permits controls to be located on either the back or side walls

Vertical Grab Bars Can Be a Safety Aid for Standing People Entering a Tub

Getting In and Out of Bathtubs

Many people who have mobility impairments have difficulty using a conventional bathtub and must learn different ways to safely get in and out of the tub.

Getting In and Out of Bathtubs

Grab Bars at Tubs

Safety for everyone is greatly increased by the addition of grab bars at bathtubs. The need for grab bars at the bathtub varies with the type and level of disability of the individual user. Some walking mobility impaired people are at great risk of falling while stepping over the tub rim. For them, a vertical grab bar which provides a stable handhold may be all that is required.

Some people who use wheelchairs can transfer from their chairs and get down into the tub independently, while others may require assistance from an attendant. For transfers, the tub may need grab bars on one, two, or all three of the enclosing walls and enough clear floor space in front to allow a forward or parallel approach.

The location of grab bars in a home will be determined by the needs of individual residents. The ANSI and UFAS standards require four horizontal grab bars at conventional tubs and three at tubs with built-in transfer seats. The ANSI/UFAS arrangement is based on averages and is good for most users. Their arrangement is especially appropriate where multiple users are expected, in rental housing for example. (Please see ANSI and UFAS for required lengths and positions of grab bars at tubs.)

It is of critical importance for safety that grab bars be carefully selected and installed. Please see "Grab Bar Installation" below.

ANSI/UFAS Grab Bar Configuration at Tubs

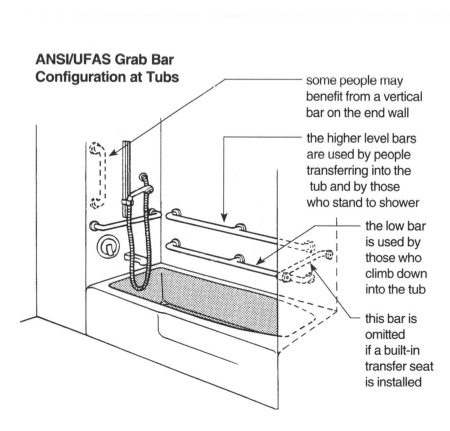

some people may benefit from a vertical bar on the end wall

the higher level bars are used by people transferring into the tub and by those who stand to shower

the low bar is used by those who climb down into the tub

this bar is omitted if a built-in transfer seat is installed

Forward Transfer from a Wheelchair into a Tub

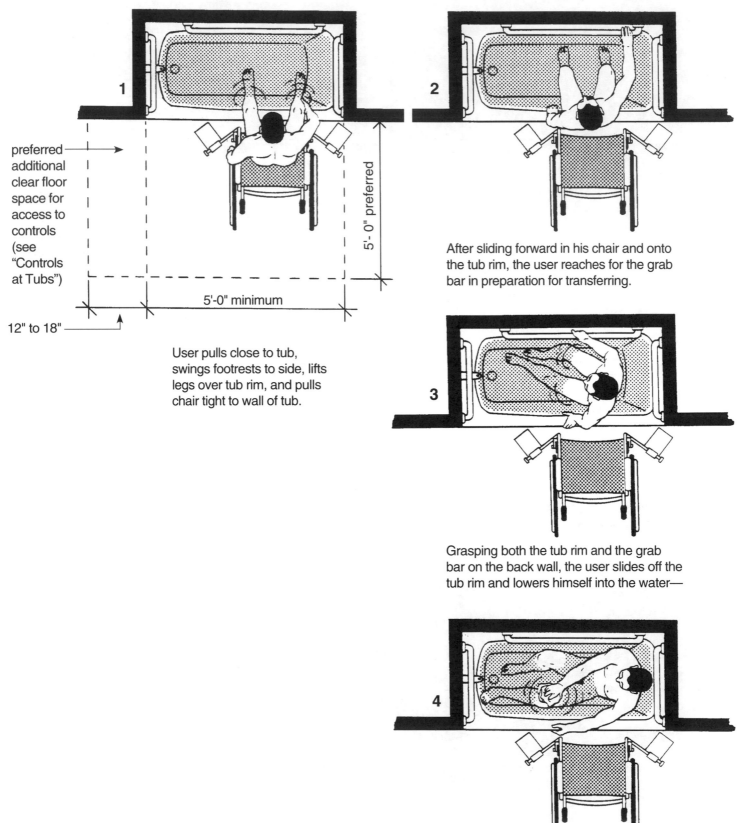

1

preferred additional clear floor space for access to controls (see "Controls at Tubs")

5'-0" preferred

5'-0" minimum

12" to 18"

User pulls close to tub, swings footrests to side, lifts legs over tub rim, and pulls chair tight to wall of tub.

2

After sliding forward in his chair and onto the tub rim, the user reaches for the grab bar in preparation for transferring.

3

Grasping both the tub rim and the grab bar on the back wall, the user slides off the tub rim and lowers himself into the water—

4

for a relaxing bath!

Getting In and Out of Bathtubs

Transfer Surface

Often a built-in transfer surface or seat at the head (opposite the control end) of the tub is necessary. This transfer surface provides a place for a mobility impaired person to sit for a moment during the process of entering the tub. The ANSI and UFAS standards call for a built-in surface that is 15" deep with enough clear floor space outside the tub to allow parallel approach with a wheelchair.

Tub with Built-in Transfer Surface

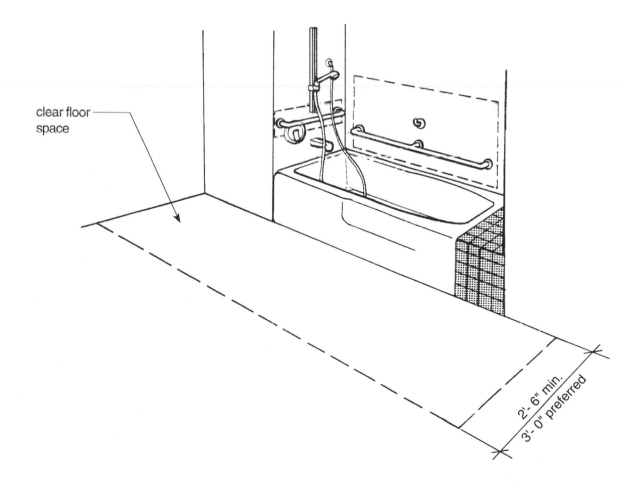

clear floor space

2'- 6" min.
3'- 0" preferred

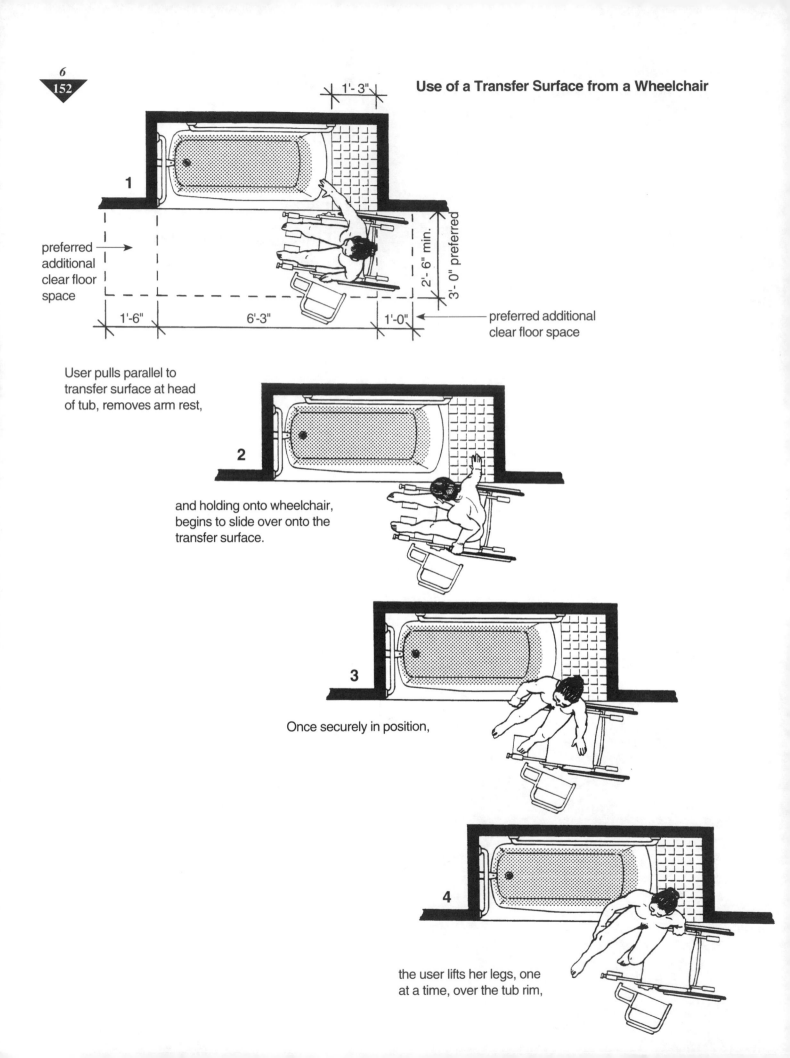

1'- 3"

preferred
additional
clear floor
space

2'- 6" min.

3'- 0" preferred

1'-6"   6'-3"   1'-0"

preferred additional
clear floor space

User pulls parallel to
transfer surface at head
of tub, removes arm rest,

2

and holding onto wheelchair,
begins to slide over onto the
transfer surface.

3

Once securely in position,

4

the user lifts her legs, one
at a time, over the tub rim,

Use of a Transfer Surface from a Wheelchair

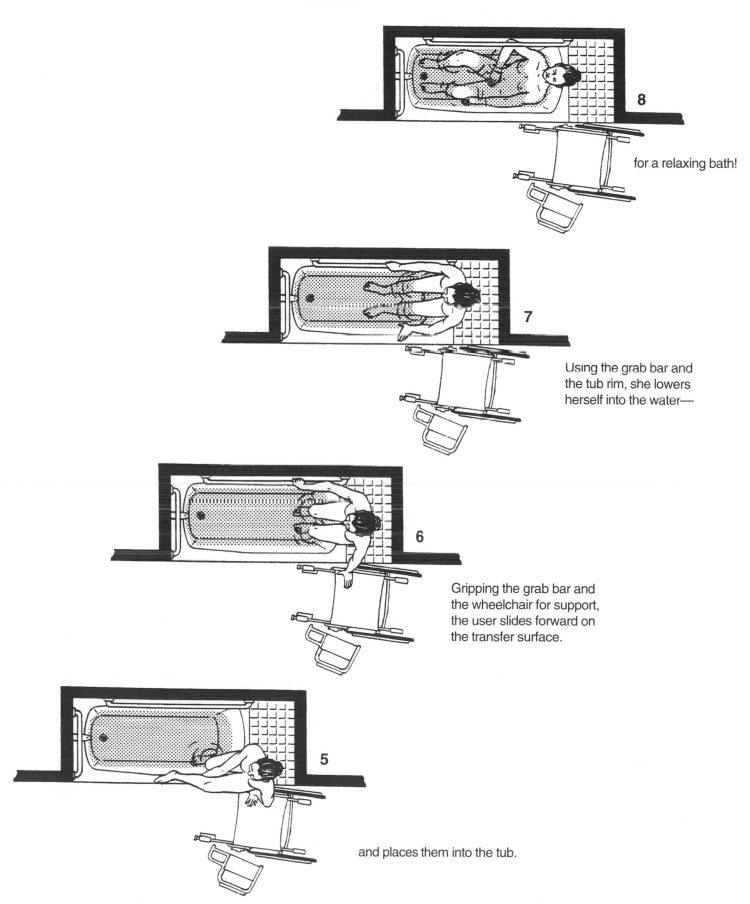

8

for a relaxing bath!

7

Using the grab bar and
the tub rim, she lowers
herself into the water—

6

Gripping the grab bar and
the wheelchair for support,
the user slides forward on
the transfer surface.

5

and places them into the tub.

Getting In and Out of Bathtubs

Transfer Surface

Walking mobility impaired people can sit down on the transfer surface before entering the tub, thereby avoiding the risk of falling while stepping over the rim.

Transfer surfaces can be built out of tile or other waterproof materials. It should be noted that transfer surfaces are not intended for use while showering. If such use is anticipated, appropriate slopes, drains, and curtains must be included.

Transfer Surface Used by Walking Mobility Impaired People

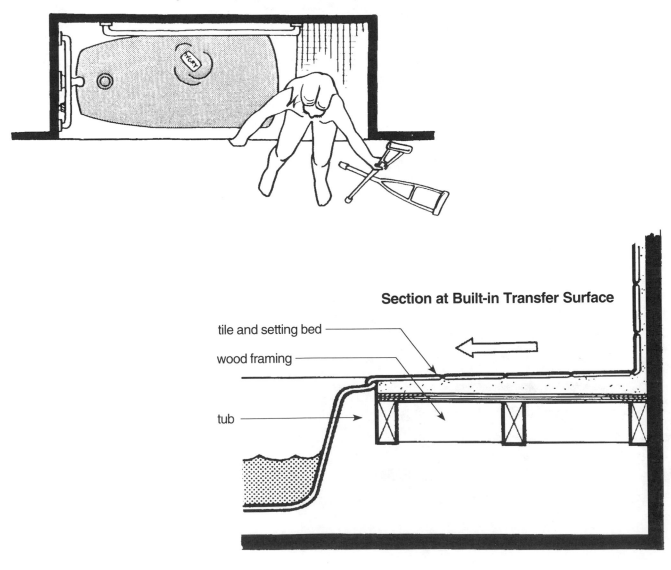

Section at Built-in Transfer Surface

tile and setting bed

wood framing

tub

Getting In and Out of Bathtubs

Hydraulic Seat

Hydraulic seats can also be used to facilitate getting into a conventional bathtub. The seats are usable by many wheelchair users and walking mobility impaired people as well.

Hydraulic seats are powered by water pressure. They raise and lower the user into the tub and some models rotate out over the tub rim when in the "up" position to make it easier for users to get onto the seat. The user must remain on the seat while bathing because the mechanism takes up space in the tub. With the seat in place, it is impossible to get all of the way down into the tub or to recline in the tub.

Some disadvantages of hydraulic seats are their weight and the fact that they must be completely disconnected and removed from the tub if other people wish to bathe without the seat.

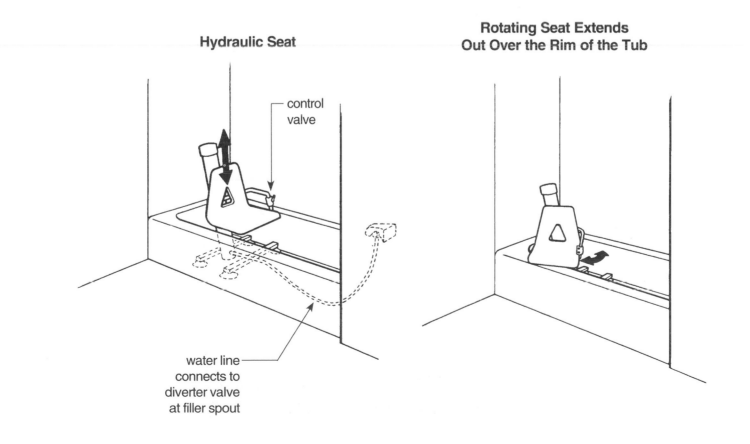

Hydraulic Seat

control valve

water line connects to diverter valve at filler spout

Rotating Seat Extends Out Over the Rim of the Tub

**Wheelchair Users Make
a Lateral Transfer onto
the Rotated Seat**

**User Operates Valve
to Lower and Raise
the Seat as Needed**

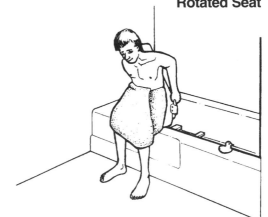

Getting In and Out of Bathtubs

Lifts at Tubs

Some people with disabilities will not be able to make a transfer and will have to be lifted into a conventional bathtub. Mechanical lifting devices can be used to avoid the risks inherent in carrying and placing someone into a tub.

**Walking People
Sit Down on the
Rotated Seat**

Hydraulic Boom Lifts

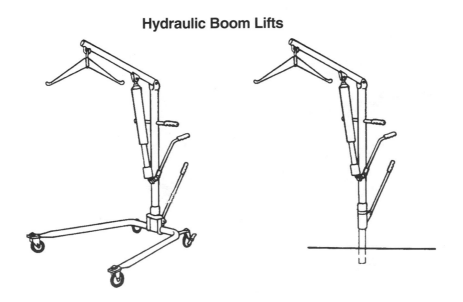

Getting In and Out of Bathtubs
Portable Boom Lifts

Portable boom lifts are common for attendant use. They can be mounted in a floor socket at a tub or on a rolling dolly. The booms are raised and lowered by an attendant who operates a lever on a hydraulic pump.

The person being lifted sits or lies upon a fabric seat or sling. The person's chair or gurney is positioned under the boom and the fabric seat is attached by chains or cables to a spreader bar which is in turn attached to the lift boom with a swiveling hook. The attendant pumps the boom up to lift the person and then manually rotates the boom to swing the person over the tub. Opening a valve on the lift gently lowers the person into the tub where the lift cables can be detached. The fabric seat may be removed or remain in the tub while bathing.

Sockets for floor mounted boom lifts must be carefully positioned before the socket is installed to be certain the lift can swing properly. The socket can be installed in existing or newly constructed houses.

The lift mechanism can be removed from the socket and placed in storage when not in use. However, the lifts are heavy and cumbersome to carry, so storage should be located nearby. Because the lifts are bulky and unattractive, the best storage space would be an enclosed closet equipped with an additional floor socket to store the lift upright, maximizing available storage space.

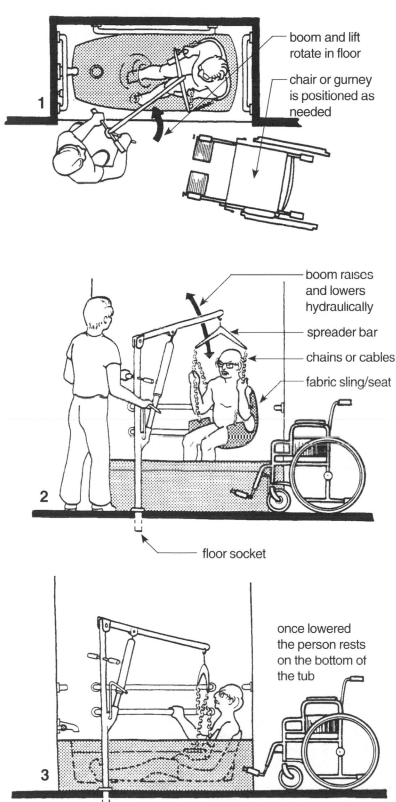

Use of a Portable Boom Lift at a Bathtub

1. boom and lift rotate in floor — chair or gurney is positioned as needed

2. boom raises and lowers hydraulically — spreader bar — chains or cables — fabric sling/seat — floor socket

3. once lowered the person rests on the bottom of the tub

Getting In and Out of Bathtubs

Rolling Portable Boom Lifts

Rolling portable boom lifts are similar to those using floor sockets except they are mounted on a large stable rolling dolly. These lifts allow an attendant to pick a person up and roll them to another location. For example, someone could be picked up from the bed and rolled into the bathroom.

There must be adequate space available for a rolling portable boom lift to be used. The frame of the rolling dolly must pass under or around the bed, chair, or other surface from which the person is to be lifted. Use of portable rolling lifts at tubs is only possible when the tub is raised above the floor to provide a "toe" space for the legs of the rolling base. Since rolling boom lifts are quite large and somewhat clinical looking, an enclosed storage space near the bedroom or bathroom keeps them close at hand but out of the way when they are not being used.

Use of a Portable Rolling Boom Lift at a Bathtub

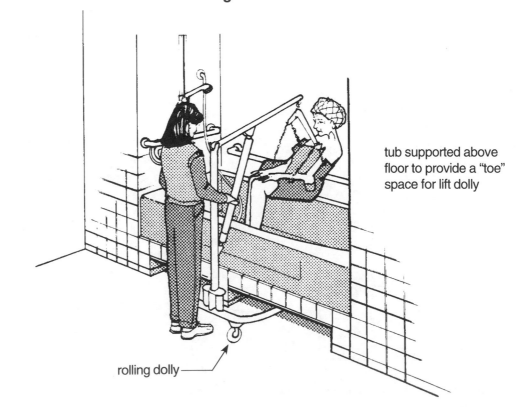

tub supported above floor to provide a "toe" space for lift dolly

rolling dolly

Use of an Overhead Track Lift at a Conventional Bathtub

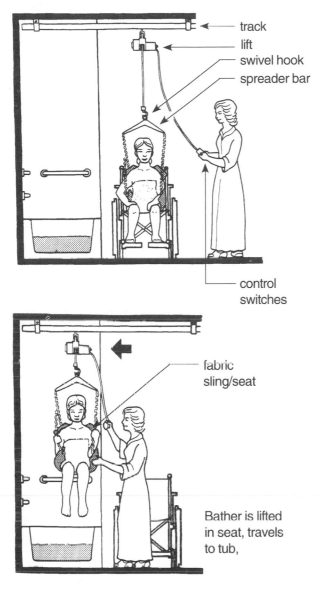

track
lift
swivel hook
spreader bar

control switches

fabric sling/seat

Bather is lifted in seat, travels to tub,

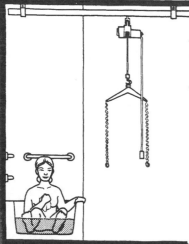

and is lowered into water where lift may be detached and moved out of way.

Getting In and Out of Bathtubs
Overhead Track Lifts

Overhead track lifts are power-operated devices that move along a track mounted in the ceiling. Using the same type of fabric sling/seat as other lifts, track-mounted lifts use electricity to power lift and move the person along the course of the track. The lifts operate on low voltage electricity to provide safety near water. They can be controlled by either the user or an attendant from a switch box on a hanging cord.

Ceiling-mounted tracks can be installed wherever they are needed and can be extended from one room to another. A track that runs between the bed, toilet, and tub allows the user to make a single transfer to the lift rather than several transfers between a wheelchair and the various fixtures. Self-operated track lifts can provide a degree of independence for some severely disabled individuals not achievable any other way.

In planning for overhead lift installations, it is a good idea to extend the track into a special closet or cupboard that can serve as a "lift garage". This will keep the machine and its components out of sight when not in use.

A Self-operated Track Lift with Storage Closet

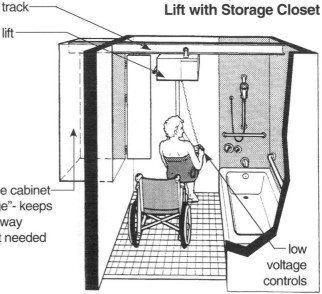

track
lift

lift storage cabinet or "garage"- keeps lift out of way when not needed

low voltage controls

Removable Seats at Tubs

Unlike the hydraulic seats and lifts which allow the user to soak in the tub, removable tub seats elevate the user to the rim height of the tub. Tub seats are useful for people who cannot get down into a tub or who do not want or cannot afford an attendant or mechanical lift. Seats mounted in tubs are in many ways similar to transfer showers, allowing the user to "shower while seated."

Many tub seats bridge the tub rim and have two legs that stand inside the tub and two legs that stand outside the tub on the floor. The portion of the seat outside the tub serves as a transfer surface and the slatted portion over the tub serves as the seat during bathing. The user first sits on the transfer surface then slides over onto the seat while transferring their legs over the rim and into the tub. Most tub seat users remain seated while showering. However, some people use the seat only to avoid the risk associated with stepping over the rim of the tub and, once in the tub, stand up to shower in the conventional manner.

This type of tub seat must be adjusted to slope inward toward the tub to prevent water from running down the frame and onto the floor. There is usually a slot between the transfer surface and the seat area through which a modified shower curtain can be threaded to help contain the water in the tub.

Typical Free-standing Tub Shower Seat

The Transfer Surface Outside the Tub Is a Convenience and Safety Feature for Everyone

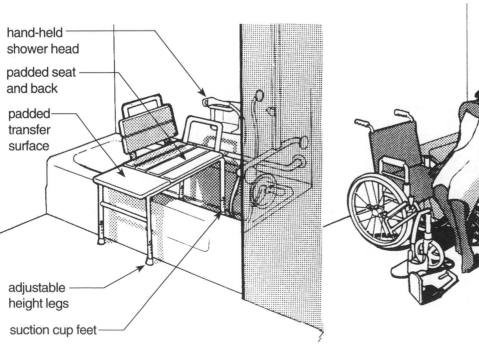

hand-held shower head

padded seat and back

padded transfer surface

adjustable height legs

suction cup feet

Removable Seats at Tubs

When choosing and installing a free-standing tub seat, precautions must be taken to ensure its stability. Usually, the legs of this type of seat have large suction cups on the bottom to promote stability. However, tub seats that attach only by suction cups are not entirely stable. The most secure free-standing seats have clamping devices that fasten tightly onto the tub. The ANSI and UFAS standards require that all seats at tubs be built-in or be capable of being securely attached to the tubs.

Tub seats should be easy to remove so the tub can be used by all members of the family. Ideally, a nearby closet could provide space to store the seat out of sight when not in use.

In response to the increasing need for seats in tubs or showers, some plumbing fixture manufacturers have models which include integral seats or they manufacture seat accessories in matching colors and materials.

Portable Tub Seats That Clamp Securely to the Tub Are Preferred

Some Tub Seats Have No Outside Transfer Surface but Still Clamp to the Tub

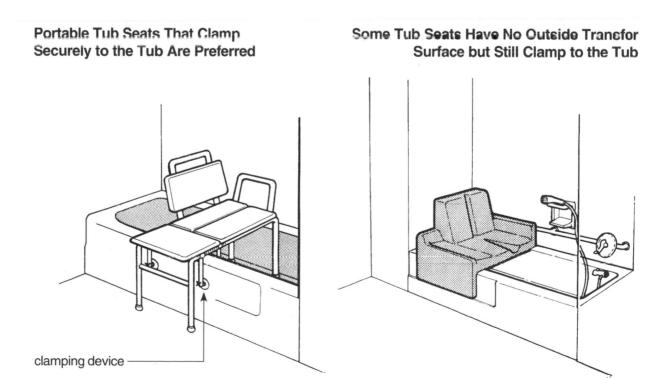

clamping device

Controls at Tubs

For controlling the water flow, valves and other controls that can be easily used with a closed fist are best. Lever handles, push plates, and electronic controls offer the preferred ease of use. Water valves, diverter valves, and other controls should be located on the end wall at the foot of the tub, below the grab bar, and offset toward the outside of the tub. This position eliminates the need to bend and stretch to reach the controls from outside the tub. Please see ANSI or UFAS for dimensions.

**Lever Handle Control
Valves Are Preferred**

ANSI/UFAS Tub Control Wall

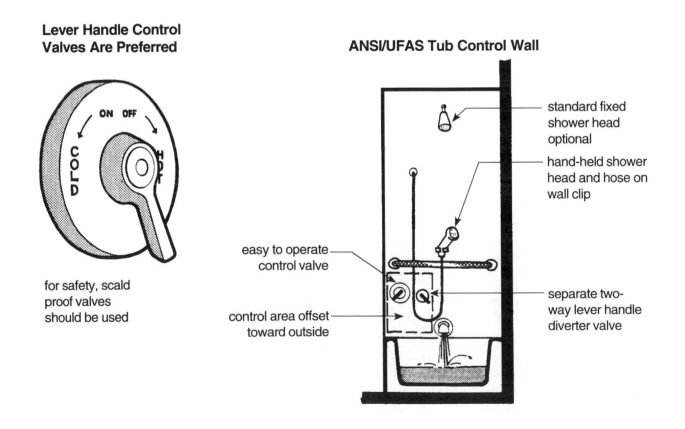

for safety, scald
proof valves
should be used

easy to operate
control valve

control area offset
toward outside

standard fixed
shower head
optional

hand-held shower
head and hose on
wall clip

separate two-
way lever handle
diverter valve

Controls at Tubs

Since many disabled people have limited skin sensation, scald-proof thermostatically controlled or pressure balanced valves should be used to control the flow of hot water. Separate lever handle diverter valves are preferred over integral push-pull devices for the flow valves. Pop-up filler spout diverters and shower head mounted diverters are not within reach of many people with disabilities and should be avoided.

Hand-held shower heads are essential at accessible tubs. Mounting clip holders should be placed on the wall or a slide-bar installed so the hand-held unit is always available just above the grab bar. It is best if both a hand-held and a standard fixed shower head are provided. In some cases, the hand-held unit can double as a fixed head by installing a second holder clip at the height of the standard head or by using a slide-bar for positioning the hand-held unit.

**Hand-held Shower Head
On a Slide-bar Mount**

Offset Control Location Is Easier for Everyone to Use

offset control location

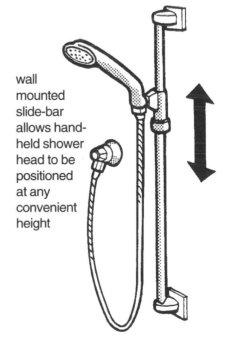

wall mounted slide-bar allows hand-held shower head to be positioned at any convenient height

an additional clear floor space of 12"-18" here allows wheelchair users to reach controls without stretching over the footrests on their wheelchair

Walking People May Choose to Sit While Showering

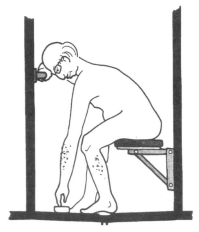

The grab bar serves as a balance point while leaning over to wash feet as well as a gripping surface for entering and exiting the stall.

This shower, with its seat, provides bathing ease for someone who walks with difficulty or who may not be able to stand to shower.

The 3' x 3' Transfer Shower
Grab Bars at Transfer Showers

The ANSI and UFAS standards require only one horizontal L-shaped grab bar in transfer showers. Some people may benefit from the installation of an additional vertical grab bar on the control wall. This vertical bar may also be helpful to standing people in maintaining balance. See ANSI/UFAS for required length and position of the horizontal bar and the section below on "Grab Bar Installation".

Because the seat folds up, the stall works as a conventional 3' x 3' shower stall.

The 3' x 3' Transfer Shower
Controls

Control valves and diverter valves for transfer showers should be similar to those described for bathtubs. In this case, however, the controls are mounted above the grab bar. Please see "Controls at Tubs".

3' x 3' Transfer Shower Control Wall

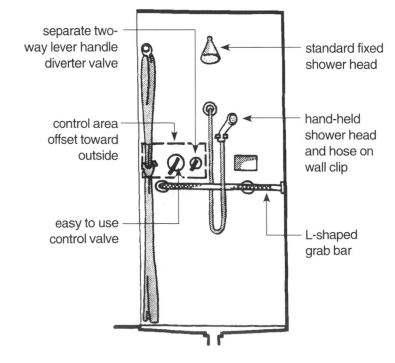

separate two-way lever handle diverter valve

standard fixed shower head

control area offset toward outside

hand-held shower head and hose on wall clip

easy to use control valve

L-shaped grab bar

ANSI/UFAS Minimum-sized Roll-in

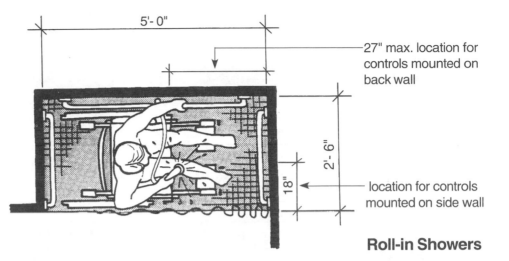

UFAS specifies controls be located on a side wall within 18" of front edge of shower. (ANSI allows controls to be placed on any of the three walls)

5'- 0"

27" max. location for controls mounted on back wall

2'- 6"

18"

location for controls mounted on side wall

Roll-in Showers

A roll-in shower is simply a waterproofed area where a person can remain in a wheelchair while showering. Generally, a special waterproofed wheelchair is used for this purpose.

The size of a roll-in shower can vary widely depending on the user's ability and the available space. The ANSI and UFAS standards permit a roll-in shower as small as 2'-6" x 5'-0". This size occupies the same space as a conventional bathtub but is considered by most experts to be too shallow to retain water. More appropriate sizes are 4' x 5' or 5' x 5'.

There should be no curbs or abrupt changes in level at the entrance to roll-in showers. A gradually sloping shower floor with a raised strip at the entrance should be used to contain water while allowing wheelchairs to roll easily and safely into and out of the shower stall.

A More Adequate Roll-in Shower

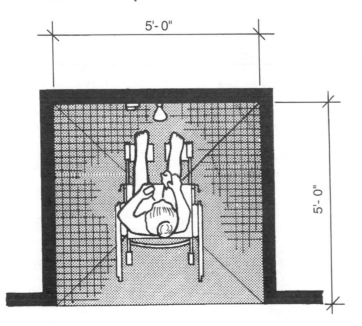

5'- 0"

5'- 0"

Roll-in Showers Are a Very Versatile Bathing Fixture

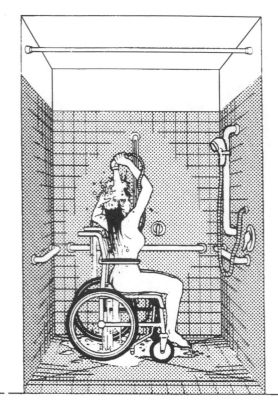

Roll-in showers provide enough space for people in wheelchairs to maneuver and enough space to have an attendant assist in the shower if necessary.

Portable seats can be placed in a roll-in shower for walking people who need to sit down to shower.

Roll-in showers can be used by non-disabled people in a conventional manner

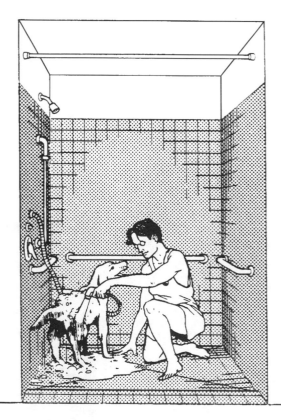

and they can be used by others for special purposes.

**ANSI/UFAS Minimum Roll-in
Shower with Extended Wet Area Floor**

**3' x 3' Transfer Shower
with Extended Wet Area Floor**

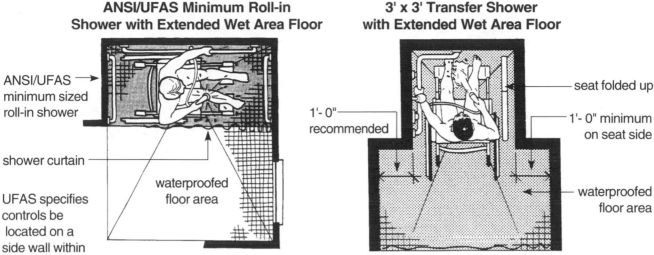

ANSI/UFAS → minimum sized roll-in shower

shower curtain

waterproofed floor area

UFAS specifies controls be located on a side wall within 18" of front edge of shower, ANSI specifies controls be placed either on side wall or forward or back of center on the back wall

seat folded up

1'- 0" recommended

1'- 0" minimum on seat side

waterproofed floor area

Roll-in Showers

Where space is limited or where smaller sized roll-in showers are planned, it may be best to simply waterproof the entire bathroom floor and let it slope gently to a drain. An entirely waterproofed "wet area" serves multiple purposes and eliminates the need to retain the water within the immediate shower stall. For example, the small and somewhat inadequate ANSI/ UFAS 2'-6" x 5'-0" roll-in shower becomes a successful roll-in if the floor outside the stall is waterproofed as well. Some people can use the 3' x 3' transfer shower as a roll-in shower if it is equipped with a folding seat, and the floor outside is waterproofed and slopes to the floor drain.

"Wet areas" can be designed to allow multiple activities to occur in one space. This double use can save space and allow more types of bathing options in one bathroom. For example, a "wet area" located outside a conventional bathtub can be used as a roll-in shower. A combination shower and toilet compartment may also work provided the toilet fixture does not interfere with wheelchair maneuvering space.

Roll-in Shower Beside a Conventional Tub

tub controls may suffice if hand-held shower hose is long enough to reach the bathing area

waterproofed floor slopes gently to drain

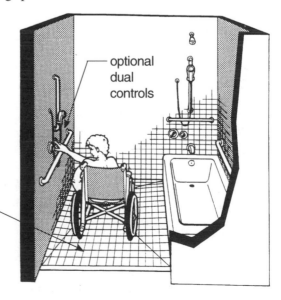

optional dual controls

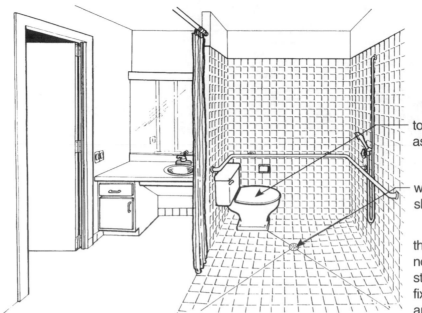

toilet can be used
as a shower seat

waterproofed floor
slopes gently to drain

this configuration may
not comply with the
standards unless the
fixtures and elements
are carefully arranged

Roll-in Showers
Grab Bars

The ANSI and UFAS standards require horizontal grab bars on all three walls of walk-in/roll-in showers. Some people may prefer installation of additional vertical grab bars on the side walls and/or adjacent to the controls. These vertical bars may be helpful to standing people in maintaining their balance as well as providing a safety measure when shower floors are slippery.

Where ANSI/UFAS compliance is required, refer to the standards for specified length and position for horizontal bars. Please also see the section below on "Grab Bar Installation".

Roll-in Showers
Controls

Control valves and diverter valves for roll-in showers should be similar to those described for bathtubs. Please see "Controls at Bathtubs".

The ANSI standards allow the controls to be mounted on both the side and back walls of the small 2'- 6" x 5'- 0" roll-in shower. The UFAS standards require that the controls be mounted on a side wall. The mounting heights of the grab bars and controls should comply with the ANSI/UFAS specifications with the operating valves placed immediately above the horizontal grab bar.

Lavatories (Sinks)

Both wall-mounted and countertop lavatories are used in accessible bathrooms. Lavatories can be standard models acquired from local vendors. Special "handicapped" models with elongated bowls are not needed and should not be used.

Although special fixtures are not necessary, certain features must exist for the lavatory to be usable. These features are as follows: 1) there must be a knee space under the lavatory so that people who use wheelchairs can pull underneath and get close enough to use the fixture; 2) there must be a clear floor space, 30 inch minimum width by 48 inch minimum depth, that extends a maximum of 19 inches under the lavatory; 3) the lavatory must have at least 29 inches of clearance from the floor to the bottom of the apron at the front of the lavatory; 4) the drain and supply pipes must be covered to protect against accidental burns; 5) faucets must be able to be operated without gripping or twisting; and 6) the mirror must be mounted no higher than 40 inches off the floor.

Knee spaces are particularly important in bathrooms which are generally small and have little maneuvering space. The knee space under the lavatory provides clearance for turns as well as space for a close approach to the lavatory by people using wheelchairs.

Characteristics of an Accessible Lavatory

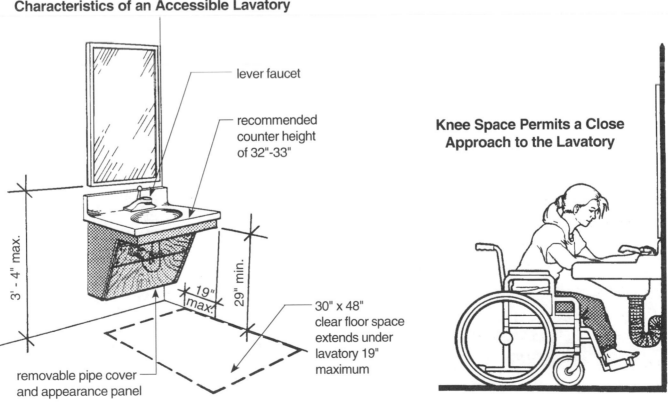

lever faucet

recommended counter height of 32"-33"

3' - 4" max.

19" max.

29" min.

30" x 48" clear floor space extends under lavatory 19" maximum

removable pipe cover and appearance panel

Knee Space Permits a Close Approach to the Lavatory

Lavatories (Sinks)

Although wall-hung lavatories can meet all of the above mentioned criteria, they are not ideal. Some disabled people must lean on a lavatory to maintain their balance. Many wall-hung lavatories will pull loose from the wall or their mounting brackets will bend under such loads. If used, wall-hung lavatories must have extra strength brackets or legs.

Because of their design, wall-hung lavatories have little if any shelf space and therefore provide no surface on which to place toiletry and personal items. This presents a difficult situation for many disabled people who have difficulty reaching up into wall cabinets for supplies or bending over to pick up items that inevitably fall off a wall-hung lavatory.

Wall-hung Lavatories Provide No Space for Toiletries and May Come Loose from Wall When Leaned On

Countertop lavatories can provide ample surface area and are generally a better choice for accessible bathrooms. Conventional countertop lavatories can be used and the counter can be any size. For use by disabled people, lavatories mounted in standard countertops, are best when placed as close as possible to the front edge of the countertop. This position allows a person to lean over the bowl more easily to wash or clean their teeth and reach to controls.

Countertops containing lavatories can be mounted on custom made wall brackets so the necessary knee space can be provided for wheelchair users. In rental housing where occupants may change frequently, the wall brackets can be surrounded by a free-standing base cabinet that will provide a vanity for tenants who do not require knee space. This "adaptable" vanity base cabinet can be removed and placed in storage when knee space is required. For additional adaptable design information please see *Adaptable Housing: A Technical Manual for Implementing Adaptable Dwelling Unit Specifications* (publication # HUD-1124-PDR).

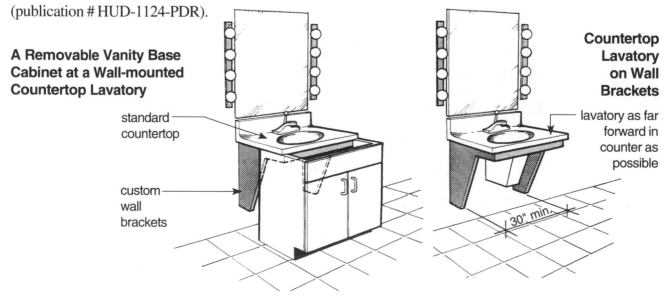

A Removable Vanity Base Cabinet at a Wall-mounted Countertop Lavatory

standard countertop

custom wall brackets

Countertop Lavatory on Wall Brackets

lavatory as far forward in counter as possible

30" min.

Single-lever or Blade Handles Are the Easiest to Operate

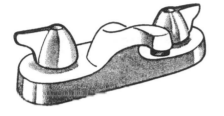

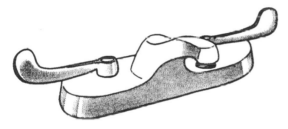

Lavatories (Sinks)
Faucets and Controls

Many people have difficulty using faucets and water controls that require grasping and twisting of symmetrical shapes such as round, cylindrical, or square faucet handles. Asymmetrical valve handles, such as lever or blade handles, are good choices because they can be used without gripping or twisting. Single-lever faucet controls are preferable because both temperature and flow rate can be adjusted with one hand in a single motion.

If a proposed faucet can be operated with a closed fist and requires less than five pounds of force to operate, it is probably an acceptable control for most disabled people.

Electronically controlled faucets are now available that sense the presence of the user's hands and automatically turn on the water. The faucets eliminate the need to touch or turn handles and the temperature and flow rate are preset. Although these faucets are primarily used in commercial settings, they may be of benefit in the home for people with severe hand limitations.

Electronically Controlled Faucets Eliminate the Need to Turn Handles

Toilets

Toilets for use by mobility impaired people are best located in a corner where the wall behind and beside the fixture can be reinforced, and grab bars can be mounted if they are needed. To provide space for a person's shoulders, 18" of clearance should be allowed between the center line of the toilet and the side wall.

There should also be ample clear floor space in front of and beside the toilet fixture to allow people using wheelchairs and walkers to maneuver, approach the seat, and make a safe transfer.

The ANSI/UFAS standards require clear floor space that varies depending upon the direction of approach to the toilet. When the fixture can be approached from both the front and the side and a lavatory is installed next to the toilet, the floor space to allow transfers must be at least 4'-0" x 5'-6". The minimum 4'-0" dimension extends into the room from the side wall next to the toilet fixture. The minimum 5'-6" dimension is measured from the wall behind the toilet to the wall in front of the toilet fixture.

When the fixture can be approached from the front or side and no lavatory is installed next to the toilet, the floor space must be at least 5'-0" x 4'-8" and extend at least 3'-6" to the side from the center line of the toilet. This provides a minimum clear space beside the toilet for users to execute side transfers.

Some people can transfer to and from the toilet from only one side. Others can complete right, left, or front transfers. The technique used depends on which approach is most familiar, easiest, and safest to complete. Whenever possible, it is best to position the toilet to allow both front and side transfers.

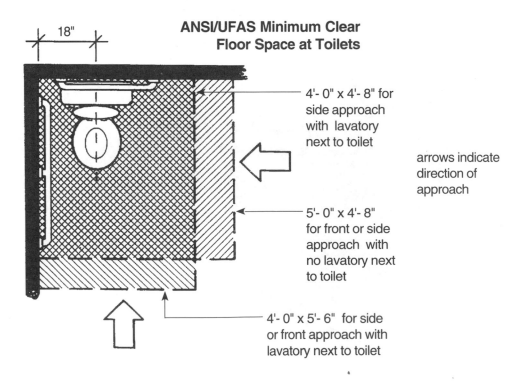

ANSI/UFAS Minimum Clear Floor Space at Toilets

18"

4'- 0" x 4'- 8" for side approach with lavatory next to toilet

arrows indicate direction of approach

5'- 0" x 4'- 8" for front or side approach with no lavatory next to toilet

4'- 0" x 5'- 6" for side or front approach with lavatory next to toilet

Minimum Clear Floor Space for Toilets with Front and Side Approach

corner installations are preferred for toilets

reinforced areas for grab bar installation as needed

bold arrows indicate direction of approach

vanity base cabinet (removed)

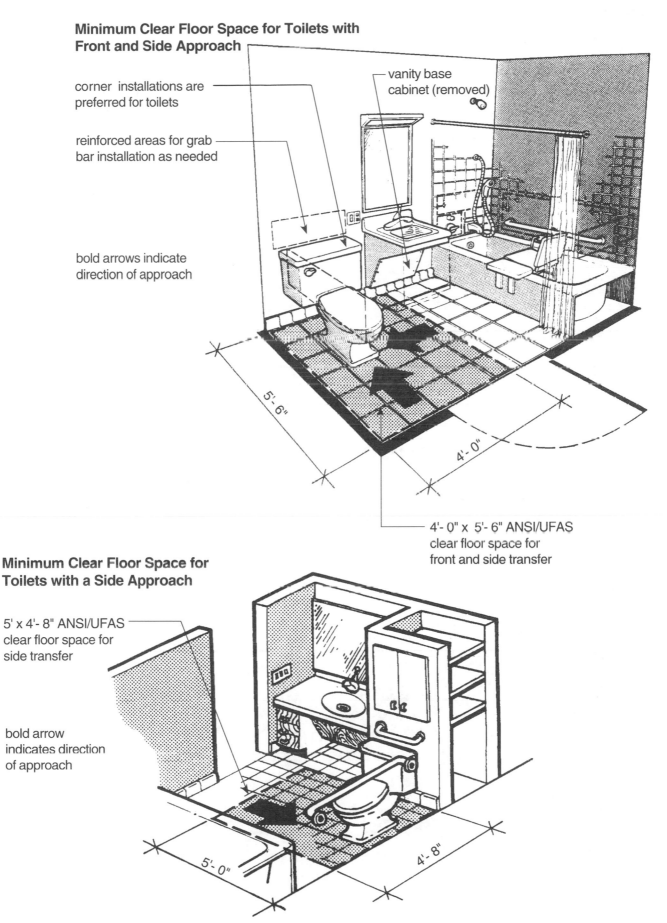

5'- 6"

4'- 0"

4'- 0" x 5'- 6" ANSI/UFAS clear floor space for front and side transfer

Minimum Clear Floor Space for Toilets with a Side Approach

5' x 4'- 8" ANSI/UFAS clear floor space for side transfer

bold arrow indicates direction of approach

5'- 0"

4'- 8"

Toilets

Getting On and Off the Toilet

Many people who use wheelchairs are unable to stand up while transferring from a wheelchair to the toilet. These users must be able to position their wheelchair close to the toilet seat to transfer onto the toilet. Wheelchair users utilize several common positions while making a sliding transfer.

Common Wheelchair to Toilet Transfer Techniques

Diagonal Approach

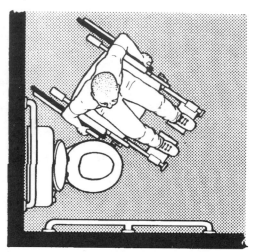

The user parks at a comfortable angle with the chair seat against the toilet.

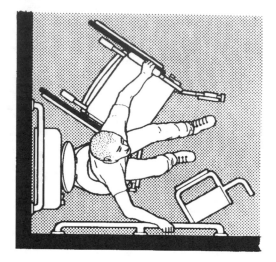

After swinging the footrests out of the way and possibly removing the armrest, the user makes a sliding transfer using the grab bars and chair for support.

Reverse Diagonal Approach

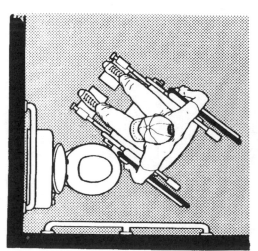

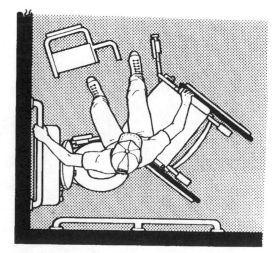

This method may be used to achieve a left-handed transfer in a right-handed room or vice versa.

Common Wheelchair to Toilet Transfer Techniques

Diagonal Approach with Attendant Assistance

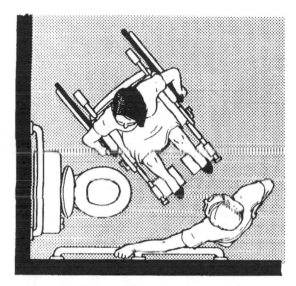

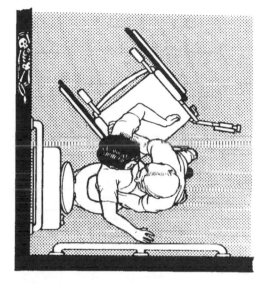

The user is positioned diagonally with the wheelchair seat close to the toilet. The attendant stands in front.

After swinging the footrest to the side, the attendant lifts the person to a standing position, rotates them, and places them on the toilet seat.

Perpendicular Approach

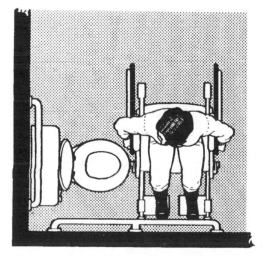

The user positions their chair at a 90 degree angle to the toilet, locating the wheelchair seat as close as possible to the toilet seat.

After removing one armrest and using the grab bar and toilet for support, the user makes a sliding and pivoting transfer onto the toilet seat.

Common Wheelchair to Toilet Transfer Techniques

Parallel Approach

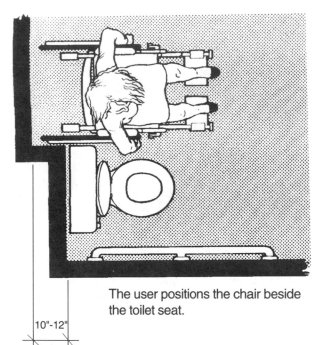

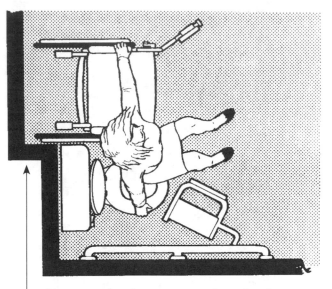

10"-12"

The user positions the chair beside the toilet seat.

After removing the armrest and rotating the footrests out of the way, the user makes a lateral sliding transfer using the grab bar and the chair for support.

Note: Offsetting the toilet wall 10" to 12" provides extra space for the rear wheels of a wheelchair so the user can position the wheelchair seat parallel to the toilet seat. A safer and easier parallel transfer can then be made.

Toilets
Seat Height

The height of a toilet seat can radically affect the use of the toilet by a disabled person. No single height is right for all users. Very low and very high seat heights are not good for anyone.

Low seats are difficult for walking mobility impaired people who have trouble getting up on their feet. They are also difficult for wheelchair users who may be able to transfer onto the seat but not get back into their wheelchairs without assistance.

High seats are better for walking people who have difficulty getting up from a seated position. However, they can be uncomfortable for shorter people because the user's feet do not touch the floor, making balancing difficult and sometimes restricting blood circulation in the legs. Wheelchair users often cannot get onto very high seats without assistance.

The ANSI/UFAS standards specify a toilet seat height for dwellings of 15" to 19". As a general rule, 18" is a good height. This dimension is the same as most wheelchair seats.

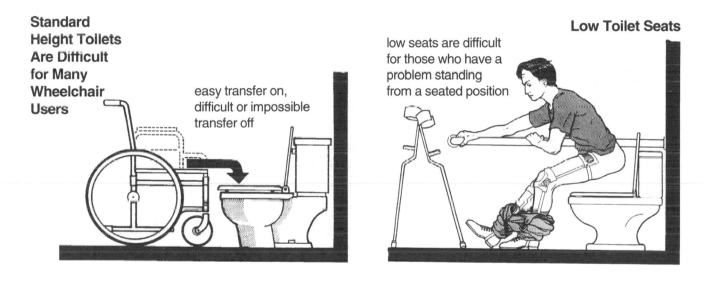

Standard Height Toilets Are Difficult for Many Wheelchair Users

easy transfer on, difficult or impossible transfer off

Low Toilet Seats

low seats are difficult for those who have a problem standing from a seated position

High Toilet Seats

high seats are uncomfortable because the user's feet often do not touch the floor which makes balancing difficult

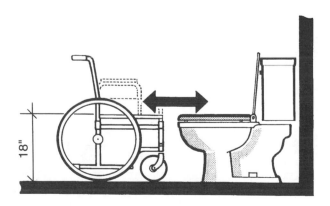

Suggested Optimum Height for Most Users

18"

Elevated Seats on Conventional Low Toilets

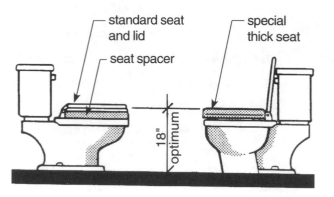

Toilets

Establishing a Specific Seat Height

There are few if any moderate height toilets available. Most are low, approximately 15" high, while some special "handicapped" units are very high, approximately 19"-20".

Special thick toilet seats can be added to conventional low toilets to provide an intermediate seat height. A spacer ring can be placed between the toilet rim and a standard seat to raise it to a particular height. Thick seats and spacer rings are available in a variety of thicknesses.

In new construction, a conventional low toilet can be mounted on a raised base to bring the seat to any desired height.

Elevated Base for Toilets

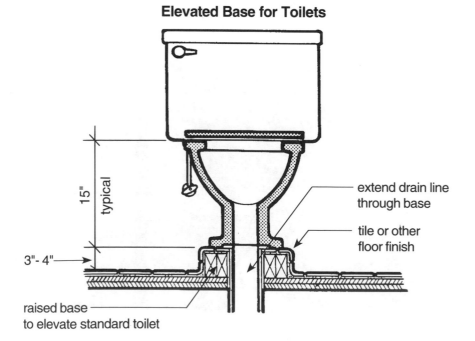

ANSI/UFAS Complying Grab Bars at Toilets

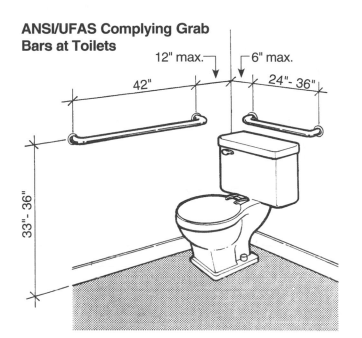

Occasionally Non-complying Grab Bars Are Used Where Space Is Limited

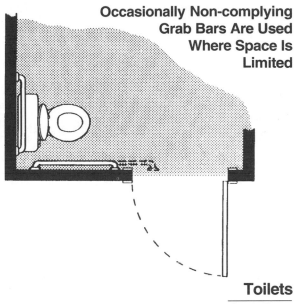

Toilets
Grab Bars

The ANSI/UFAS standards require either the installation of two grab bars or reinforcing for later installation of grab bars at toilets in dwellings. One bar must be on the wall beside the toilet and the other on the wall behind the toilet fixture. The bars are used by mobility impaired people when transferring onto and off of the toilet and to maintain balance while seated on the toilet.

The side-mounted bar is required by ANSI/UFAS to be a minimum of 42" long and the rear-mounted grab bar is required to be a minimum of 24" or 36" long. Grab bars should be mounted on a reinforced wall at a height of 33"-36" from the floor (see "Grab Bar Installation").

Seat-mounted Grab Bars

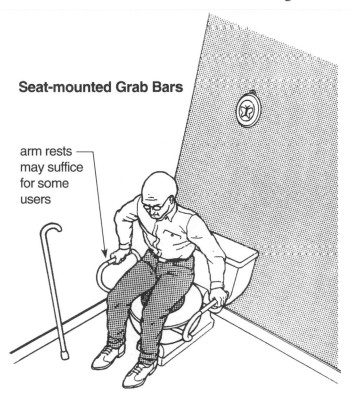

arm rests may suffice for some users

In small bathrooms where a door is located in the side wall, immediately adjacent to and forward of the toilet, a full length ANSI/UFAS complying grab bar may not be possible without enlarging the room. In such instances some people substitute a shorter grab bar. While this shorter grab bar is not preferred, it does work for many people. If shorter bars are used, they should be custom fitted over the door jamb and trim in order to achieve maximum length.

Some people who walk with difficulty and have problems sitting down and getting up again may benefit from seat-mounted grab bars that provide armrests on both sides of the seat. These bars bolt to the toilet fixture and work well as an aid to many older people. They generally do not work well for wheelchair users who cannot stand up while transferring.

Grab Bar Installation

Grab bars are used around toilets, bathtubs, and showers to provide grasping and support surfaces. They help people maintain balance while transferring from a wheelchair or while sitting down from a standing position. People also rest their arms on grab bars to reach controls or to maintain balance, especially when they have limited grasping ability.

Grab bars must be firmly attached and capable of supporting 250 pounds of force in any direction. In new frame construction, the bars must be attached either to studs or to wall reinforcing/blocking mounted behind the finished wall surface. Do not attach a grab bar to an existing stud wall without providing some additional reinforcing because the bar will not support enough load.

When it is necessary to add a grab bar on an existing wall that does not have reinforcing, two approaches can be taken: 1) the existing finish on the wall can be dismantled and reinforcing added in the area where the grab bar is to be located, or 2) exposed reinforcing can be installed by attaching a board to at least two studs and then attaching the grab bar to the board. The board must be securely attached to the studs and it is preferred that at least one end of the grab bar also be attached through the board to a stud. Although not recommended, if this solution is used in bathtub and shower areas, the board and fasteners must be waterproofed.

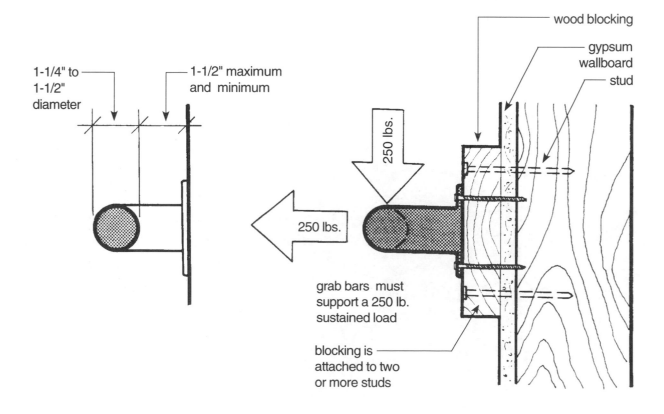

Grab Bar Diameter and Mounting Distance from Wall

Surface Applied Reinforcing for Mounting Grab Bars

Grab Bar Installation

The ANSI and UFAS standards require specific areas to be reinforced for grab bars. Solid wood blocking is best for this purpose. When fiberglass or plastic tub and shower walls are used, the blocking should be shaped and extended to fit tightly against the plastic wall so no gap exists between the wall of the fixture and the house studs.

Some people may need or benefit from a grab bar or handle in a location that is unique to their way of bathing. For this reason, it is a good idea to reinforce entire wall areas around the bathtub, shower, or toilet, allowing for the addition of other grab bars later if needed. Whole wall reinforcing can be accomplished by providing a structural plywood reinforcing panel as back-up to the regular finish wall material.

Reinforcing for Grab Bars Behind Fiberglass or Acrylic Tub and Shower Surrounds

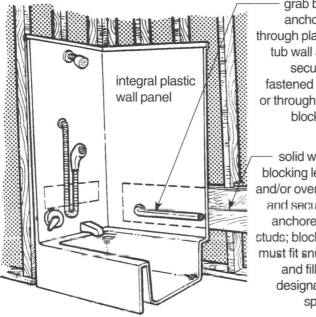

integral plastic wall panel

grab bars anchored through plastic tub wall and securely fastened into or through the blocking

solid wood blocking let-in and/or overlaid and securely anchored to studs; blocking must fit snugly and fill the designated space

Whole Wall Plywood Reinforcing for Grab Bars on Stud Walls

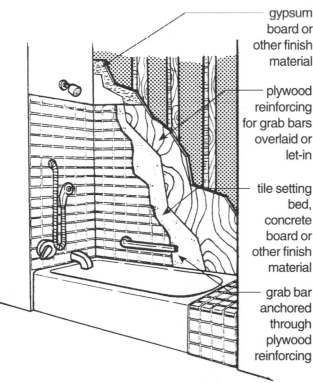

gypsum board or other finish material

plywood reinforcing for grab bars overlaid or let-in

tile setting bed, concrete board or other finish material

grab bar anchored through plywood reinforcing

Solid Wood Reinforcing for Grab Bars on Wood Stud Walls

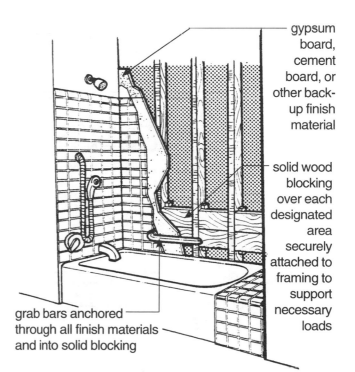

gypsum board, cement board, or other back-up finish material

solid wood blocking over each designated area securely attached to framing to support necessary loads

grab bars anchored through all finish materials and into solid blocking

Grab Bar Installation

The space between a grab bar and the wall must be exactly 1-1/2". A wider gap is dangerous because the user's arm may slip through the space between the wall and the bar resulting in loss of balance, and possible arm fracture, if a fall were to occur. A smaller gap does not allow ample space for user's hands and knuckles.

Grab bars are now available in a variety of shapes, colors, and materials, including metal, nylon, and plastic. Some are decorative and can double as towel bars. Others are furnished as an integral part of molded shower or tub fixtures. Grab bars can also be custom made to suit individual preferences or design styles.

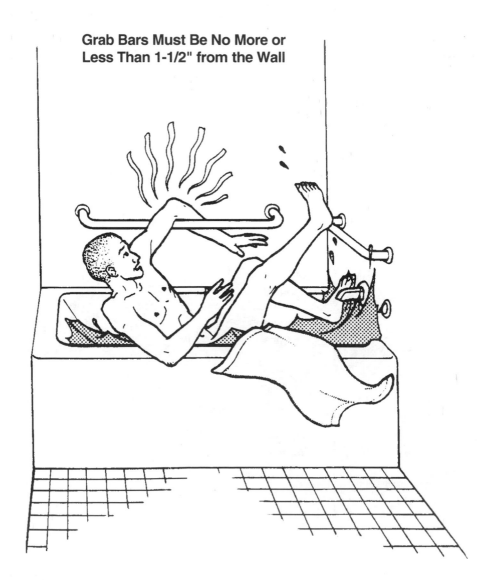

Grab Bars Must Be No More or Less Than 1-1/2" from the Wall

Small Bathroom with a Transfer Shower

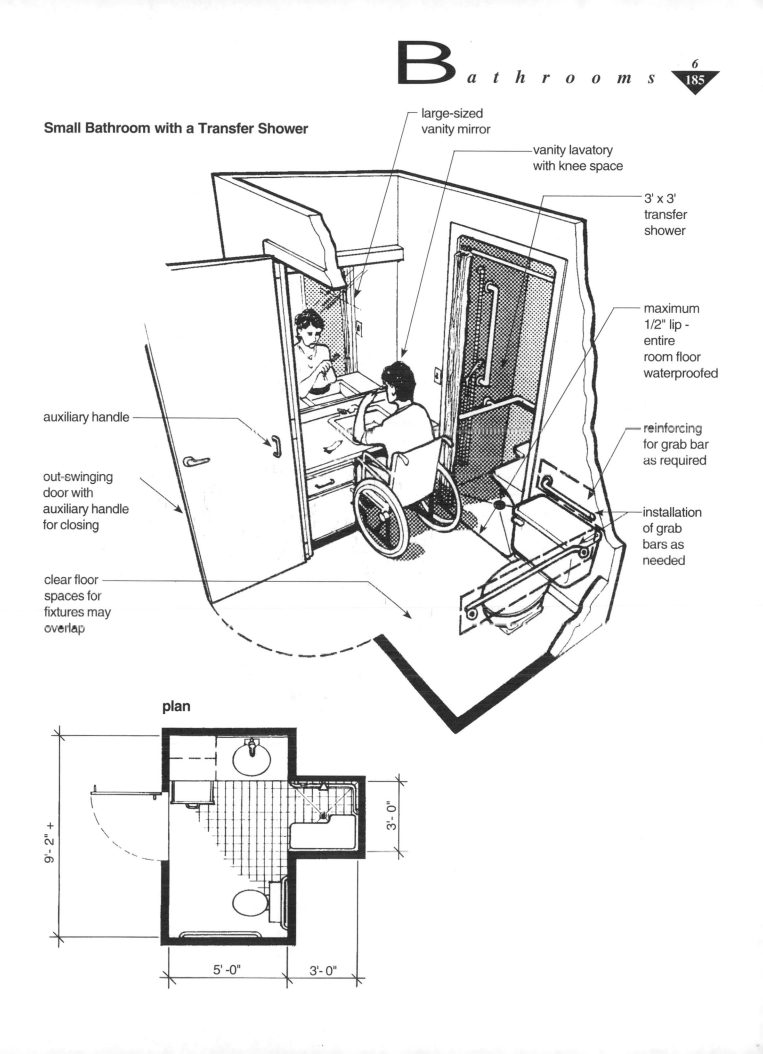

large-sized vanity mirror

vanity lavatory with knee space

3' x 3' transfer shower

maximum 1/2" lip - entire room floor waterproofed

reinforcing for grab bar as required

installation of grab bars as needed

auxiliary handle

out-swinging door with auxiliary handle for closing

clear floor spaces for fixtures may overlap

plan

9'- 2" +

3'- 0"

5' -0"

3'- 0"

Bathroom with Built-in Transfer Surface at Tub

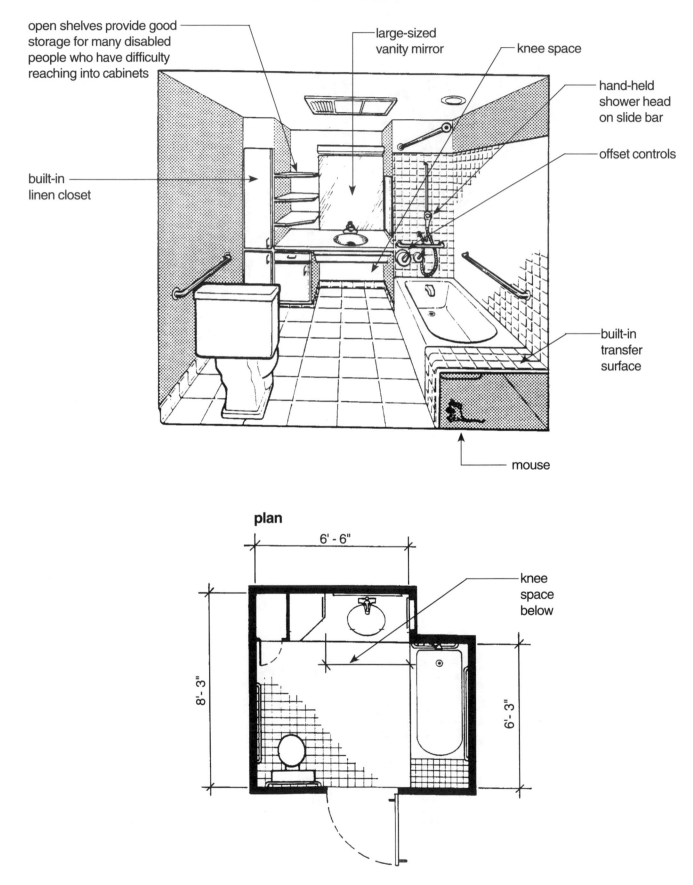

open shelves provide good storage for many disabled people who have difficulty reaching into cabinets

large-sized vanity mirror

knee space

hand-held shower head on slide bar

offset controls

built-in linen closet

built-in transfer surface

mouse

plan

6' - 6"

8' - 3"

6' - 3"

knee space below

Combination Laundry and Bathroom with Roll-in Shower

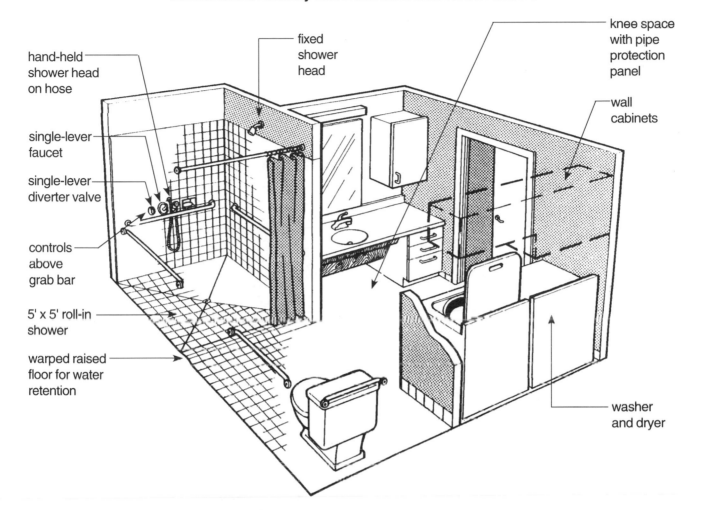

hand-held shower head on hose

single-lever faucet

single-lever diverter valve

controls above grab bar

5' x 5' roll-in shower

warped raised floor for water retention

fixed shower head

knee space with pipe protection panel

wall cabinets

washer and dryer

Plan with Roll-in Shower

Alternate Plan with Tub

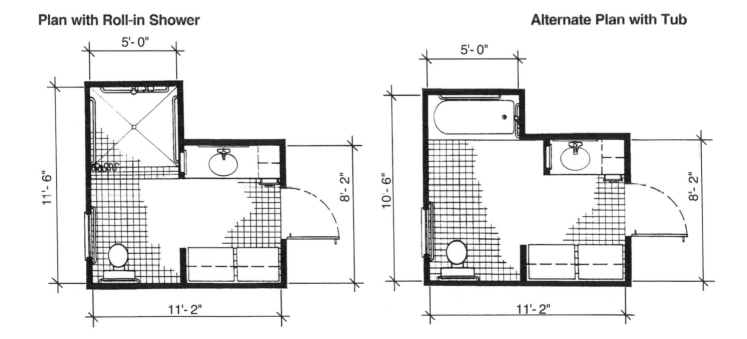

5'- 0"

11'- 6"

8'- 2"

11'- 2"

5'- 0"

10'- 6"

8'- 2"

11'- 2"

B *e d r o o m s*  189

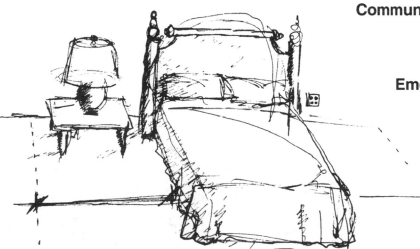

continued on next page

▲

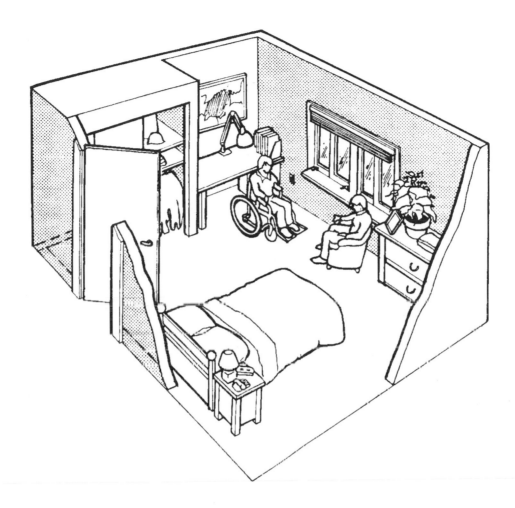

Accessible Bedrooms

Many disabled people are able to use bedrooms of conventional design. However, bedrooms for use by mobility impaired people (people who use wheelchairs, walkers, crutches, or canes) have significant space requirements and need to be planned carefully so they may be used independently. Ideally, all spaces and features of the room should be useable by the occupant. Access to doors, windows, closets, beds, and other furnishings can be achieved when particular attention is given to providing adequate maneuvering space and clearances as well as appropriate assistive devices. These topics should be carefully considered during initial space planning.

Specific information on doors and windows is available elsewhere in the *Design File*. The remaining topics are discussed in detail on the following pages.

Room Size

Accessible bedrooms can be of almost any size. The appropriate size depends on the resident's disability type, the amount and type of furnishings, and the degree of independent use preferred. Other factors affecting room size are costs and convenience for companions and caregivers.

Maneuvering Space and Clearances

Accessible Route

The minimum clear width for wheelchair passage is 3'-0". At least 3 feet of width should be provided between pieces of furniture and between walls and furniture where passage is desired. This clear path with no abrupt changes in level greater than 1/4" is known as an accessible route.

An accessible route can turn 90 degrees. However, at the minimum 3'-0" width, the passageway is very tight and it is difficult for some people using wheelchairs to make a 90 degree turn without hitting the wall. For this reason, at 90 degree turns it is preferred that one leg of the space be at least 3'- 6" wide.

**Minimum Width for
a Wheelchair to Pass**

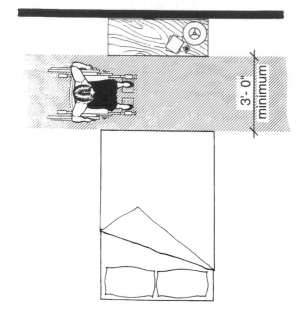

**Minimum Width Too Narrow for Some
People When Making a 90 Degree Turn**

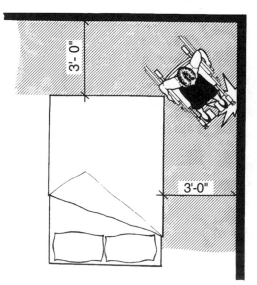

**Larger Space Preferred for
One Leg of a 90 Degree Turn**

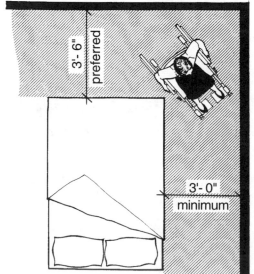

Maneuvering Space and Clearances
Turnaround Space

The 3'- 0" accessible route or aisle space does not provide enough space for wheelchair users to turn around. It is possible to plan a room with an "accessible route" that would require the person to back out. However, maneuvering a wheelchair in reverse for more than a few feet is difficult or impossible for many people. To create a more useable room, a bedroom plan should include at least one turnaround space.

There are two types of turnaround spaces. A 5'-0" diameter circle and a T-shaped space. The circular space allows a person in a wheelchair to make a pivoting turn. The 3' 0" x 3'- 0" T-shaped space allows a three point turn to be made similar to that made by an automobile, pulling into a driveway and backing out to go in the opposite direction. One leg of the T-turn could utilize either the space in a doorway or the clear knee space under a table, desk, or countertop. This arrangement can be used well where space is limited.

5' Diameter Turning Space

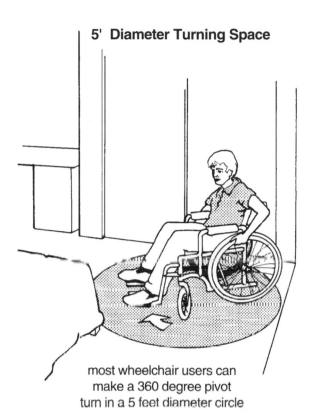

most wheelchair users can make a 360 degree pivot turn in a 5 feet diameter circle

T-turn Space at Kneespace

T-Turn Space

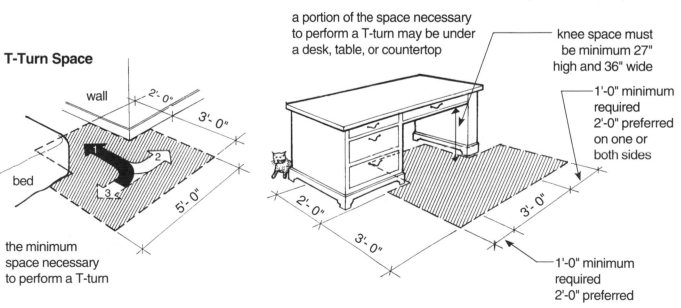

wall

2'- 0"

3'- 0"

bed

5'- 0"

3

the minimum space necessary to perform a T-turn

a portion of the space necessary to perform a T-turn may be under a desk, table, or countertop

knee space must be minimum 27" high and 36" wide

1'-0" minimum required 2'-0" preferred on one or both sides

2'- 0"

3'- 0"

3'- 0"

1'-0" minimum required 2'-0" preferred

Maneuvering Space and Clearances

Clear Floor Space for Reaching from Wheelchairs

A minimum clear floor space of 2'- 6" x 4'- 0" is needed in front of any feature that must be reached by wheelchair users. This includes light switches, window controls, thermostats, drawers, and shelves. Clear floor spaces for reaching must be served by, or be part of, an accessible route or a turnaround space. The clear floor space can be positioned parallel to the item for side reach or perpendicular to the item for forward reach. In most cases a parallel or side reach position is best because the user is closer to the item thus reducing the required reach.

Accessible routes, clear floor spaces for reaching, and turning spaces must overlap or connect with each other. In planning an accessible room, it is always best to develop a furniture arrangement plan to insure that all features, spaces, and controls are useable and within easy reach.

**Perpendicular Clear Floor
Space Position for Forward Reach**

**Parallel Clear Floor
Space Position for Side Reach**

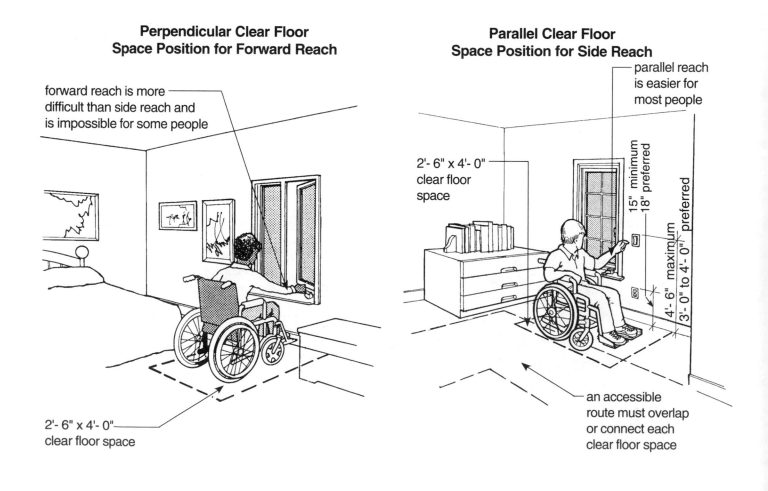

forward reach is more difficult than side reach and is impossible for some people

2'- 6" x 4'- 0" clear floor space

parallel reach is easier for most people

2'- 6" x 4'- 0" clear floor space

15" minimum
18" preferred

4'- 6" maximum
3'- 0" to 4'- 0" preferred

an accessible route must overlap or connect each clear floor space

Maneuvering Space for Unassisted Transfers

Many disabled people who use wheelchairs need extra space around the bed to position their chairs for transferring between the bed and the wheelchair. There are two basic approaches to make unassisted transfers onto a bed, the lateral transfer and the forward transfer.

For both types of transfers, it is best if the bed height is the same as the wheelchair, 18 inches is average, but this may vary. Beds can be adjusted in height by cutting legs off or by placing them on large wood blocks. If necessary, the bed covers can be arranged to conceal the wood blocks.

Lateral and forward transfer techniques are described in detail below.

Maneuvering Space for Unassisted Transfers
Lateral Transfers at Beds

**Parallel Clear Space for
Lateral Transfers at Beds**

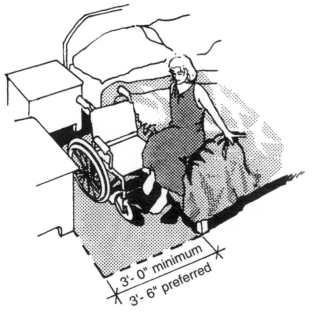

3' - 0" minimum
3' - 6" preferred

A lateral transfer requires a clear floor space parallel to the side of the bed. This space must be at least 3' - 0" wide, although a 3' - 6" space is preferred because it will allow a wheelchair user to maneuver and position their wheelchair at whatever angle is needed.

The person parks their wheelchair and locks the brakes. Usually the armrest is removed and then a sliding or pivoting transfer is made onto the bed. To bridge the gap between the seat and the bed some people may use a sliding board.

Maneuvering Space for Unassisted Transfers

Forward Transfers at Beds

Some people can only make a front or forward sliding transfer from a wheelchair to a bed. The front transfer requires a minimum 3'- 0" x 4'- 0" clear floor space, placed perpendicular to the side of the bed, although a 4'- 0" x 4'- 0" or 5'- 0" x 5'- 0" space is preferred. The user approaches the side of the bed, pulls as close as possible to the bed, and places their feet on top of the bed. On many wheelchairs, the foot rests can be unlatched and removed or swung to the side so the wheelchair seat can be drawn tight against the side of the bed. The individual can then wriggle forward out of the chair and onto the bed. The process is reversed to get out of bed.

Perpendicular Clear Floor Space for Forward Transfers at Beds

minimum 3'- 0" x 4'- 0" clear floor space, 4'- 0" x 4'- 0" or 5'- 0" x 5'- 0" preferred

Space Considerations for Assisted Transfers

Some severely disabled wheelchair users cannot make unassisted transfers onto beds and require the assistance of an attendant. Attendants may lift the person or use several transfer techniques including partial lifting. In some cases, a mechanical lift may be best for safety. For assisted transfers, the space around the bed must accommodate the wheelchair user, the wheelchair, the attendant, and if necessary, the lift device.

Portable boom lifts and overhead track lifts are two of the most common assistive devices used.

Space Considerations for Assisted Transfers
Boom Lifts

Boom lifts have a hydraulic or mechanical mechanism that raises or lowers a boom to transfer a person. Usually the person is securely positioned in a fabric sling or seat. The sling is then attached to the boom.

Boom lifts can be mounted on a rolling frame for use in different locations. Some of the rolling frame lifts are designed and carefully balanced to provide both transfer assistance and transport from one location to another.

Boom lifts can also be placed in a floor socket beside the bed. Additional fixed sockets can be installed in other locations where the lift may be needed. Sockets can be installed in new construction or added to an existing space.

Because of the size of these lifts, storage space should be planned for the lift when it is not in use. A large walk-in closet works well for this purpose.

Boom Lift on Rolling Base

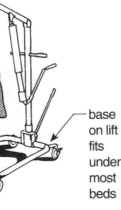

lift used to move person from one location to another

base on lift fits under most beds

Boom Lift in Floor Socket

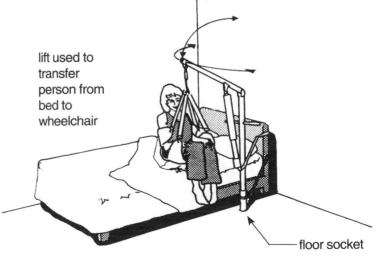

lift used to transfer person from bed to wheelchair

floor socket

Space Considerations for Assisted Transfers

Overhead Track Lifts

Overhead track lifts have an electrically operated lift mechanism that travels on a track secured to the ceiling. The lift is operated by activating buttons on a hanging switch box. Track lifts utilize the same type of fabric slings or seats as boom lifts. After the lift hoists the person, an attendant pushes or pulls the sling causing it to roll along the track in order to position the person over the bed or wheelchair.

Some track lifts have power traversing motors as well as lifting motors. The traversing motor propels the sling along the track. The entire operation is controlled from a single switch box which travels with the individual, allowing for completely independent operation.

Track lifts are more expensive than other lifts but they are generally safer, more convenient, and may be user operated. Through careful planning, the tracks can be extended into an adjacent bathroom so the same lift can be used for transfers onto the toilet and in and out of the shower or tub.

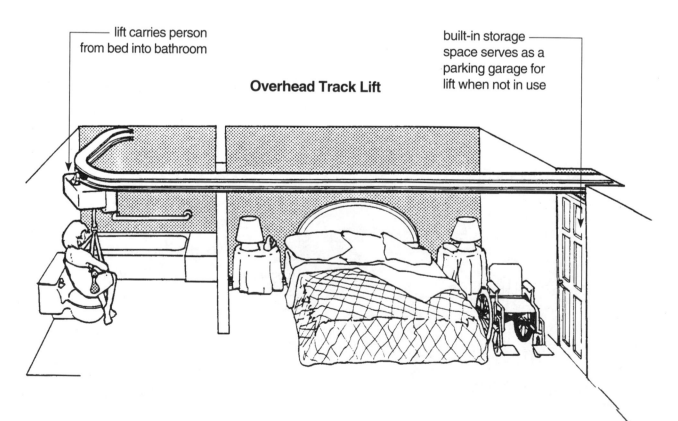

lift carries person from bed into bathroom

built-in storage space serves as a parking garage for lift when not in use

Overhead Track Lift

Space for Making Up Beds

Because many disabled people live independently and do their own household chores, it is necessary to provide adequate space for maneuvering around a bed for changing the linens and/or making up the bed. At least a 3'- 0" clear access aisle is necessary on all three sides of the bed.

Communications and Control Systems

For safety and convenience, it is important to locate telephones, light switches, emergency call buttons, other environmental control systems, and alarm controls (if any are needed) within reach from the bed. This is true for all people, but is a very important safety consideration for mobility impaired people.

Electrical Outlets at Beds

Additional electrical receptacles at the head and side of the bed are generally necessary because many disabled people use a variety of assistive devices which may be power operated. Some people use power wheelchairs or scooters which require overnight charging. Power lifts, adjustable beds, alternating pressure bed pads, oxygen concentrators, and ventilators may also be used and may require simultaneous access to electrical outlets. In addition, there are the usual electric blankets, radios, clocks, and lamps which compete for electrical outlets. An ample number of outlets should be located near the bed in an accessible place on the wall.

Additional Considerations at Beds

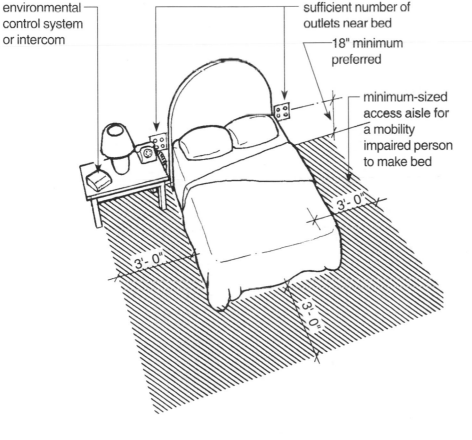

environmental control system or intercom

sufficient number of outlets near bed

18" minimum preferred

minimum-sized access aisle for a mobility impaired person to make bed

3'- 0"

3'- 0"

3'- 0"

Emergency Exits from Bedrooms

Some severely disabled people need considerable time to get out of bed and put on their prostheses or get into their wheelchair. Many dress while lying down and some must put on braces or body supports before sitting up, making response time during an emergency longer.

If possible, an emergency exit door from the bedroom to the outside should be provided. This exit door can save valuable time in getting to safety. The emergency door will also give fire rescue personnel an access route for evacuation.

A second alternative is to provide two interior accessible routes from the bedroom. The resident could leave through the alternate exit should the primary exit be obstructed. If installation of a second doorway is not possible then windows can be used for egress. Refer to the "Windows" section of the *Design File* for additional information on this topic.

Emergency Exits from Bedrooms

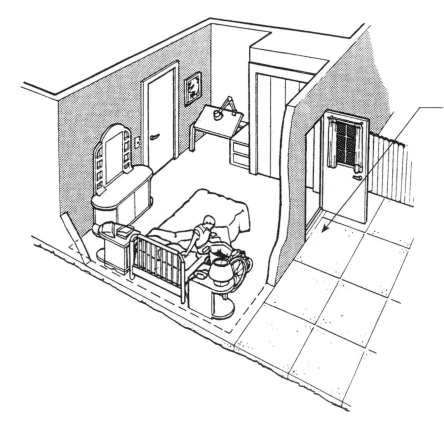

direct access to out of doors from bedroom (see "Doors" section of *Design File*).

In the event of a fire, this area should be on an accessible route so a mobility impaired person could get a safe distance from the house (see "Site and Entrances" in the *Design File*).

Closets

Closets of almost any size and configuration can be made usable for mobility impaired people provided doors are wide enough for wheelchair access. Shelves, hangers and drawers should be within a comfortable reach range for seated as well as standing people. Clear floor space should be adequate to accommodate turning and maneuvering in front of closets.

Hanging closets for clothes are usually 2'- 0" deep and of variable width depending on available space, costs and other features. The standards permit doors on shallow closets to be less than the 32" minimum clear width necessary for passage. However, it is best for accessibility for all closets to have at least a 32" clear opening.

Closets

Small Closets

A 32" minimum clear door opening should be provided into small hanging closets to allow easy reach to the entire closet contents. It is best if the closet is positioned in the room so that the closet door can swing back 180 degrees to allow maneuvering space for wheelchair users to make a diagonal approach for a side reach.

Small Closets with Minimum Width Doors

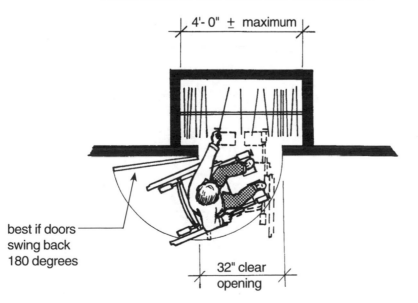

4'- 0" ± maximum

best if doors
swing back
180 degrees

32" clear
opening

Closets

Wide Closets

Wide closets with narrow doors create dead areas that many disabled people cannot reach. Wider or full width doors, which provide more than the minimum 32" clear opening, are preferred because when standing open they provide a full view of the closet contents. These doors also increase maneuvering space for wheelchair users and facilitate both left and right handed reach to the clothing. This is important because some people cannot reach forward and need to turn slightly to one side or the other to get close enough to execute a side reach. In these cases, a 4'-0" or 5'-0" wide door is preferred and will allow a full parallel or side approach.

Bi-fold and double doors are good choices for closets because they provide wide clear openings when standing open. Bi-fold doors do not protrude out into the room as far as double doors and may be a better choice where maneuvering space in front of closets is limited.

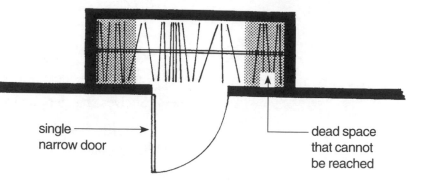

Wide Closet with Narrow Door Difficult to Use

single narrow door

dead space that cannot be reached

Wide Closet with Wide Doorway Easy to Use

double wide doors provide space for angled approach and allow left or right handed reach to contents

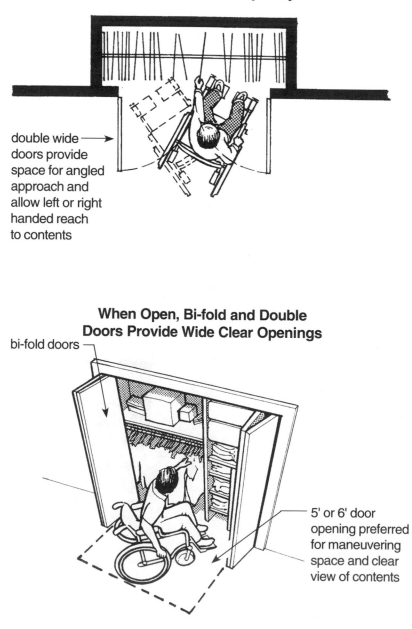

When Open, Bi-fold and Double Doors Provide Wide Clear Openings

bi-fold doors

5' or 6' door opening preferred for maneuvering space and clear view of contents

Walk-in Closets Provide Both Front and Side Access to Contents

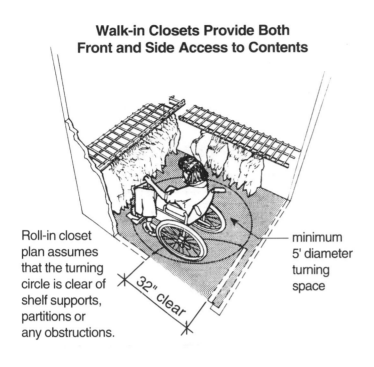

Roll-in closet plan assumes that the turning circle is clear of shelf supports, partitions or any obstructions.

32" clear

minimum 5' diameter turning space

Closets

Walk-in/Roll-in Closets

If "walk-in" closets are planned, they should be large enough to also be used as "roll-in" closets by wheelchair users. A 5'-0" diameter clear turn around space must be available inside roll-in closets. The turning space may extend 1'-0" under the clothes.

Roll-in closets do not require wider or double doors because the interior turn around space provides ample access for reach to the closet contents. A door which allows the minimum 32" clear opening for wheelchair passage is sufficient. Depending on the interior storage configuration of the closet, the door may swing either in or out. In-swinging doors should not block access to clothes storage. Common "L", "U" and parallel closet rod/ storage configurations in roll-in closets can provide ample maneuvering space for forward or side reach for almost any user.

Closet doors should meet all criteria for doors. (See "Doors" section in the *Design File* for additional information.)

Minimum Suggested L-Shaped Roll-in Closet Plan

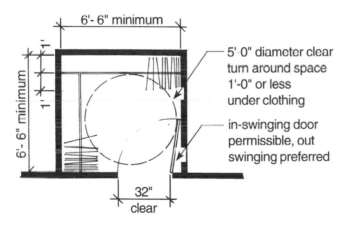

6'- 6" minimum

6'- 6" minimum

1'

1'

5'-0" diameter clear turn around space 1'-0" or less under clothing

in-swinging door permissible, out swinging preferred

32" clear

Minimum Suggested Parallel Roll-in Closet Plan

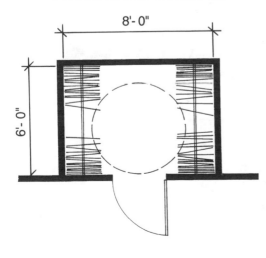

8'- 0"

6'- 0"

Minimum Suggested U-Shaped Roll-in Closet Plan

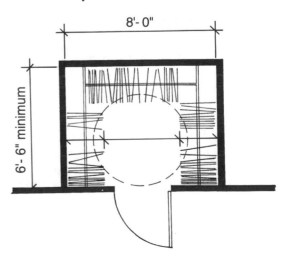

8'- 0"

6'- 6" minimum

Equipment Storage in Closets

Many disabled people have an assortment of assistive/medical equipment and often prefer that it be stored out of sight. Large closets with wide doors should be considered for storage of special equipment such as shower wheelchairs and portable lifts when they are not in use. When necessary, shelves, hooks, hanging devices, or special sockets should be installed to store the equipment in an orderly and easily accessible manner.

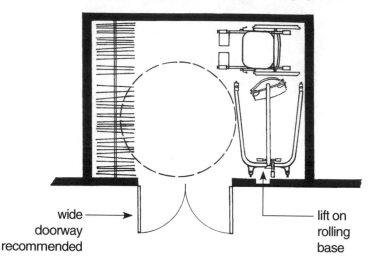

Roll-in Closet with Extra Space for Equipment

wide doorway recommended

lift on rolling base

Small Storage Closets

Small shallow storage closets, for linens and supplies, can have narrower doors as it is not necessary to provide clearance for a person to pass. However, it is best if doors on such storage closets swing back 180 degrees so wheelchair users can make a close, parallel approach for side reach to the contents.

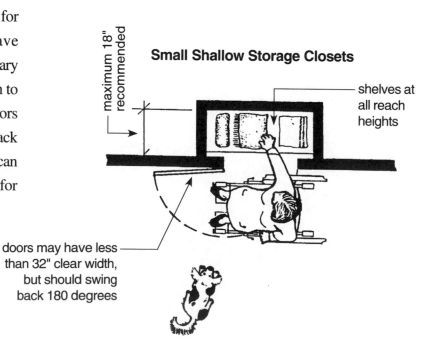

maximum 18" recommended

Small Shallow Storage Closets

shelves at all reach heights

doors may have less than 32" clear width, but should swing back 180 degrees

Storage Heights for Seated People

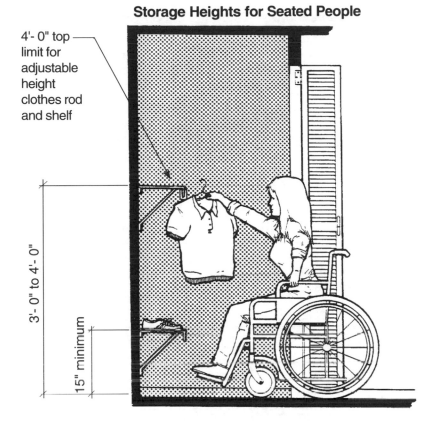

4'- 0" top limit for adjustable height clothes rod and shelf

3'- 0" to 4'- 0"

15" minimum

Storage Heights for Standing People

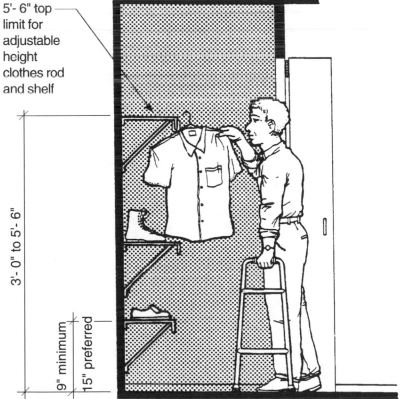

5'- 6" top limit for adjustable height clothes rod and shelf

3'- 0" to 5'- 6"

9" minimum

15" preferred

Heights for Closet Storage

The possible reach range for wheelchair users making a side reach is 9" to 4'- 6" above the floor, while the upper range for a forward reach is 4'- 0". 4'- 6" is too high for many and 9" is too low for others. A good range of heights for storage is 15" to 4'- 0" above the floor.

In rental housing where the occupants are likely to change frequently or in any housing where the occupant's ability is likely to change over time, due to aging or disability, adjustable height closet rods and storage shelves should be installed. They should be adjustable in a range from 3'- 0" to 5'- 6" above the floor so they can be lowered or raised as needed for standing and seated people.

Adjustable Storage Using Notched Rod Supports

Heights for Closet Storage

Adjustable storage can be custom built for hanging clothes. One simple approach is to use notched wood rod supports to provide different mounting heights. Two supports are installed for each clothes rod height. The height of the rod can be changed by moving it from one set of supports to another.

A combined closet shelf/clothes rod can also be made adjustable by hanging the rod from the bottom of the shelf and providing supports for the entire unit at different heights.

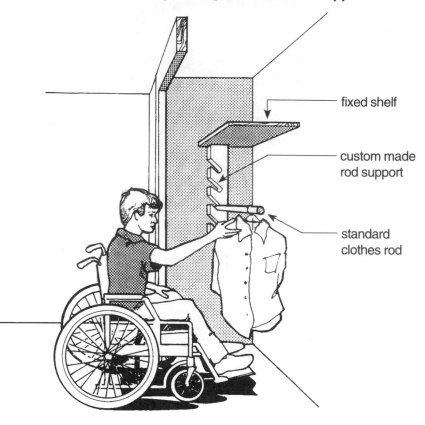

Adjustable Storage Using Notched Rod Supports

fixed shelf

custom made rod support

standard clothes rod

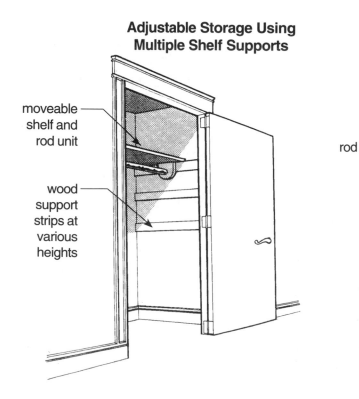

Adjustable Storage Using Multiple Shelf Supports

moveable shelf and rod unit

wood support strips at various heights

Shelf and Rod Unit

rod support

Commercially Made
Adjustable Ventilated Storage System

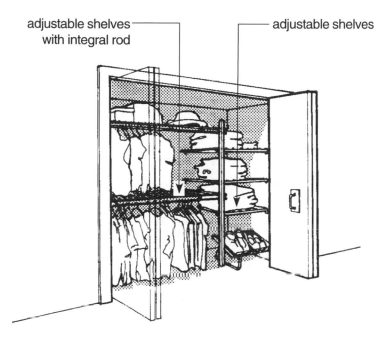

adjustable shelves
with integral rod

adjustable shelves

Heights for Closet Storage

Commercial products are also available that permit shelves and clothes rods to be added, removed, or relocated. The most common type of commercal product is the vinyl coated ventilated shelving system. Shelves with integral clothes rods can be attached to wall-mounted clips or frames and located at any height. These modular systems have many add-on components such as shelves, baskets, and hook accessories which add versatility to the system. As such, the components can be positioned to best suit the needs of the individual.

Storage Drawers that Pull Out
Fully into the Room Are Preferred

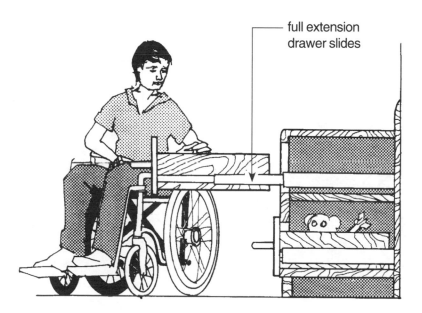

full extension
drawer slides

Storage Drawers

If built-in storage drawers are planned, it is best if they are hung on full-extension drawer slides. The slides allow the drawers to be pulled completely out of the cabinet for unobstructed viewing and reach to the contents.

Seated people cannot see over the tops of drawers if they are more than 3'- 6" above the floor. Open sided drawers, wire basket drawers, or drawers with perforations in the sides can provide a view of the contents.

Sample Bedrooms

The room arrangements depicted in the following illustrations are based on several factors including the size of the room, the type of furniture, the size and location of the closets and windows, and necessary circulation spaces. The plans are offered as samples to demonstrate how the concepts discussed in this section of the *Design File* relate to each other.

Features of Accessible Bedrooms

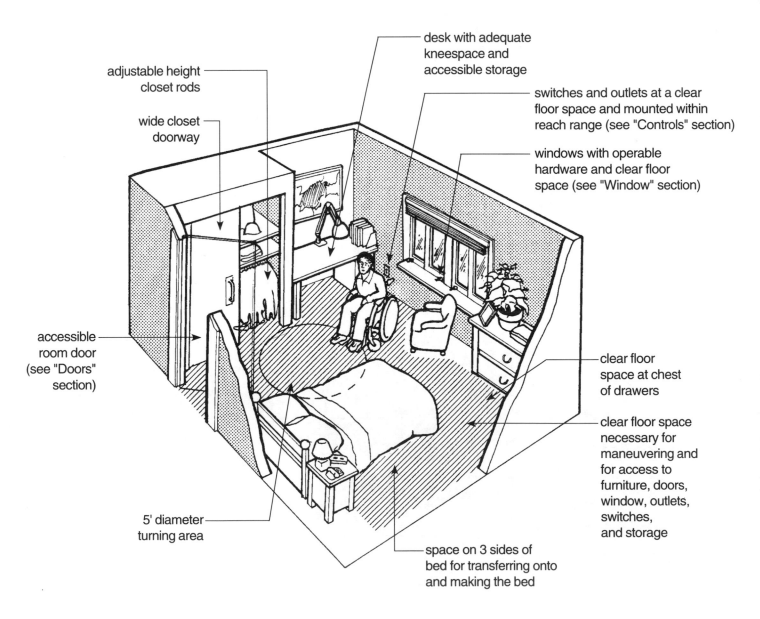

adjustable height closet rods

wide closet doorway

desk with adequate kneespace and accessible storage

switches and outlets at a clear floor space and mounted within reach range (see "Controls" section)

windows with operable hardware and clear floor space (see "Window" section)

accessible room door (see "Doors" section)

clear floor space at chest of drawers

clear floor space necessary for maneuvering and for access to furniture, doors, window, outlets, switches, and storage

5' diameter turning area

space on 3 sides of bed for transferring onto and making the bed

Sample Bedrooms

The suggested arrangements should not be interpreted as specific designs for any particular user. The accessible features and elements discussed in the *Design File* should be selected, amended as necessary, and incorporated into the most reasonable and functional plan for the users being served.

**Small Bedroom with Twin Bed, Minimal
Clear Floor Space, and Limited Access to the Bed**

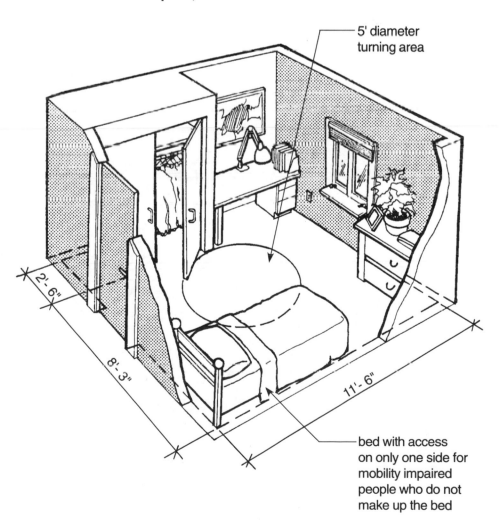

5' diameter
turning area

2'-6"

8'-3"

11'-6"

bed with access
on only one side for
mobility impaired
people who do not
make up the bed

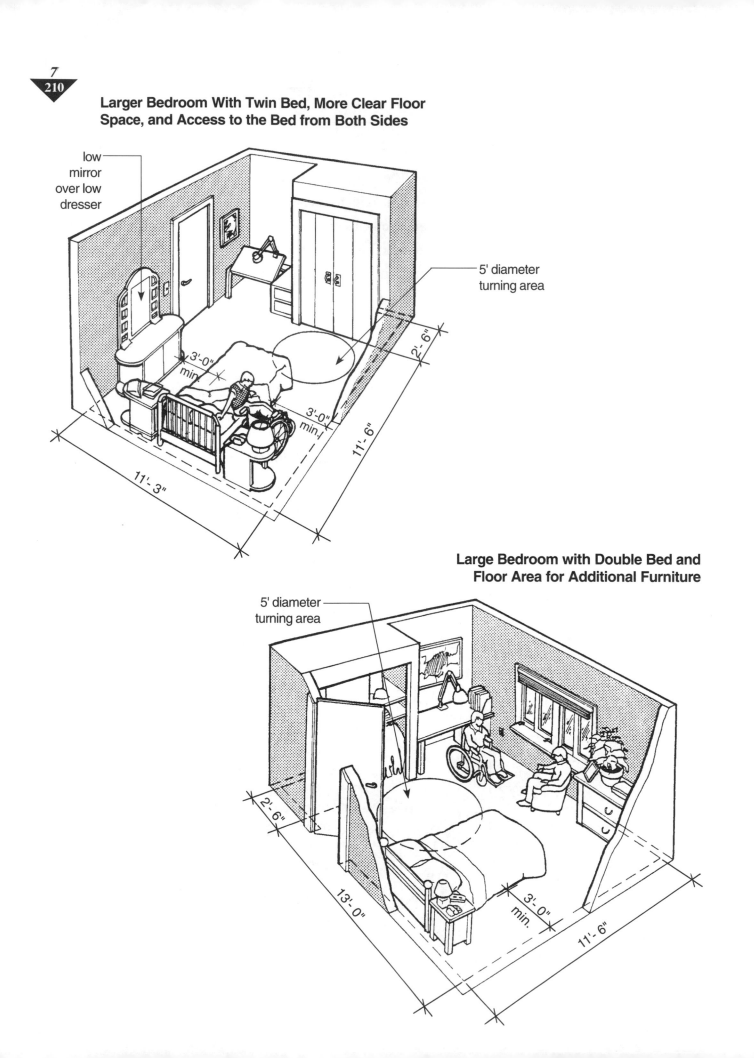

**Larger Bedroom With Twin Bed, More Clear Floor
Space, and Access to the Bed from Both Sides**

low
mirror
over low
dresser

5' diameter
turning area

3'-0"
min.

3'-0"
min.

2'- 6"

11'- 6"

11'- 3"

**Large Bedroom with Double Bed and
Floor Area for Additional Furniture**

5' diameter
turning area

2'- 6"

13'-0"

3'-0"
min.

11'- 6"

INDEX